TER

AN O ... RODUCTION

FEATURING

Roy Chiao: Father
Dennis Chan: Preacher
Crystal Kwok: Ah Choi
Stuart Ong: Cadre
Mary Walter: Amah

Director of Photography	John McCallum
Camera Assistant	Kenny Lamm
Edited by	Heinz Fussle
Original Music	Tom Howard
Script Consultant	Anthony P. B. Lambert
Production Coordinator	Chris Woehr
Written & Directed by	Bill Myers
Produced by	Heinz Fussle
Distributed by	Open Doors and Gospel Films, Inc.

***

Bamboo in Winter was launched on 1 February 1991. It was filmed entirely on location in Hong Kong and was produced by Heinz Fussle Productions of Warsaw, Indiana, USA, and was written and directed by Bill Myers of Southern California.

The film features major actors from theatrical film productions in Asia. It is based on real-life episodes in the life of the suffering house church in China, both before and after the Tiananmen Square freedom revolt in June 1989.

There is a major original musical score by Tom Howard, winner of several Dove Awards and currently recording artist on the Myrrh label.

Bamboo in Winter is available on 16mm film and in public performance video rental versions, through Open Doors and throughout the worldwide network of Gospel Films libraries and film outlets.

BAMBOO IN WINTER

The Story of the Film Release
Bamboo in Winter

DAVID PORTER

*Based on an original screenplay and
storyline by Bill Myers*

MarshallPickering
An Imprint of HarperCollins*Publishers*

Marshall Pickering is an Imprint of
HarperCollins*Religious*
Part of HarperCollins*Publishers*
77–85 Fulham Palace Road, London W6 8JB

First published in Great Britain
in 1992 by Marshall Pickering

1 3 5 7 9 10 8 6 4 2

A catalogue record for this book is
available from the British Library

ISBN 0 551 02570 0

Phottypeset by Intype, London
Printed and bound in Great Britain by
HarperCollins*Manufacturing* Glasgow

CONDITIONS OF SALE

A MESSAGE FROM
BROTHER ANDREW

(Founder and President of Open Doors International)

In today's world, the most populous continent is Asia; and in Asia, the largest nation is China. There for more than forty years the Chinese people have been indoctrinated into believing that there is no God, and that they must put all their faith in and trust in the system, in the regime and in its leaders.

But what do we see today? A tremendous restlessness is sweeping over the country, affecting everybody, but especially the youth, the students. The political system in which they have believed for so long is not only collapsing, it has actually turned against them. In despair they are now saying: 'Is there still anything that we can believe in? Is there any purpose to life?' The hunger that has thereby been created is a spiritual hunger that can only be satisfied by the precious word of God.

This is the situation in which the suffering house church is living in China. Many of the incidents in the film *Bamboo in Winter* are based on actual events. But keep in mind as you see the film, or read its story in this book that the problems faced by the Christians – the house churches, their members and their leaders – are as vast and varied as the country itself.

My prayer is that you would ask, after reading this book or seeing the film, 'Lord, what can *I* do, to help China? What can *I* do to encourage the Christians there?

What can *I* do to give the precious word of God to those who hunger for your word because they want at last to have something to live for, something they can believe in with all their hearts?'

Brother Andrew

ACKNOWLEDGEMENTS

This book is a novelization of the film *Bamboo in Winter*, details of which can be found in the preceding pages. It follows the story of the film closely, but the opportunity has been taken to provide background to the story in a way that is not possible in a film treatment.

I would like to thank Open Doors International for their advice and encouragement, and Bill Myers for commenting on a draft version. I have also benefited from the discussion with a number of individuals who have visited China and Hong Kong in recent years, and I have been particularly helped by my recollections of conversations with the late Stephen Wong, a Chinese evangelist who would have recognised many of the situations in *Bamboo in Winter*.

China is a vast country and a vast number of books have been written about it. Of the ones I have consulted I have found particularly useful those by Tony Lambert (consultant to the film project) *The Resurrection of the Chinese Church* (Hodder and Stoughton, 1991), of which I have made considerable use; by David Bonavia *The Chinese: a Portrait* (Penguin Books, rev. edn 1989); Bishop Stephen Neill's monumental and enthralling *A History of Chinese Missions* (Penguin Books, 1964); and Volume 7 of A. J. Broomhall *Hudson Taylor and China's Open Century: It is not Death to Die!* (Hodder and Stoughton and Overseas

Missionary Fellowship, 1989). All four are highly readable and I recommend them for further study.

The historical information and opinions in the present book are additional to the film content, and though they have been examined and approved by representatives of Open Doors before publication they remain the author's contribution and should not therefore be taken as necessarily expressing the emphases and opinions of Open Doors International. I am grateful to Open Doors and others for permission to use material included in the appendices.

Spelling of Chinese names has been modernized throughout: thus Mao Tse Tung becomes Mao Zedong and Peking becomes Beijing. Although this inevitably looks rather strange to many English readers, it is now the universally preferred method of transliteration and in fact gives a much better idea of the spoken sound of the Chinese name than does the earlier system.

The story of the film takes place in an unnamed Chinese village not far from Guangzhou, in May–June 1990.

THE PRINCIPAL CHARACTERS

Ah Choi, a young woman in her early twenties, has recently returned home after graduating from Beijing University, where she witnessed the crushing of the student demonstration in Tiananmen Square, Beijing, in June 1989.

Soon she will be told where the government has decided she is to work. In the meantime she is helping her father in the home and on the farm, and looking after her ailing grandmother – Amah. Her mother died when she was a baby.

Amah is very old and extremely frail. She is a devout Christian, and has talked about Jesus to Ah Choi all her life. Both Ah Choi and her father have always honoured her out of respect and affection. She has sent for the Preacher, who was at one time a close friend of the family; she needs a miracle and he has been known to perform them. Physically helpless, she is a woman of fire and determination – especially when the Gospel is being attacked.

Cho Ling is Ah Choi's father, a man in his mid-forties, and very close to his daughter. Work on the farm is hard, for the crops have been poor this year. His has been a hard life, with many unresolved loose ends. His face shows it. His comfort is wine, which he drinks too freely – Ah Choi believes that began when her mother died. Like most of the villagers, he has an ambiguous relationship with

The Cadre, who is the local village overseer. A resident of the village, he is well rewarded for his work, which includes reporting to his Party superiors about any 'counter-revolutionary' activities. He has ambitions for wealth and power, and is compromised by the graft and corruption that goes with getting it. Most villagers want to have him on their side, but few like him. He is attracted to Ah Choi and would like to marry her, but she does not reciprocate his feelings.

The Preacher is an itinerant, and has in the past had some dealings with Cho Ling, though what they are we do not know at the beginning of the story. He is like many itinerant preachers in China today; constantly harassed by the authorities, his activities are very closely monitored, and conversions will result in extreme government opposition.

All the details of his activities described in the story are taken from real-life situations. The events of the climax of the story actually happened in a rural Chinese village less than two years before the film's release.

The Pastor of the Three-Self Church is not necessarily a bad man and may be a Christian. But like many of his fellow-pastors he is hopelessly compromised by the inextricable links between his Church and the atheistic government. In a crisis he would obey the government. The Preacher has no place in the Three-Self scheme of things.

The Three-Self Church, Public Security Bureau officials and other Party and government agencies and representatives are described more fully in the appendices to this book.

CHAPTER I

In the bamboo a light wind was stirring, like a hundred pens scratching on rough rice paper, like somebody slowly turning the pages of a great book. It was going to be a hot day. Among the village houses the geese were stalking in line, their feathers already drying after their morning swim; a dog, its tongue lolling in the heat, watched them enviously. Villagers gossiped to each other as they went about their morning tasks. The familiar village smells hung in the air: the odour of refuse in the open drain, a mixture of animal smells, and occasional cooking fragrances.

Inside the house Cho Ling sat alone at table, contemplating a bottle of wine and an empty glass. He sighed heavily and picked up the bottle, recklessly splashing the wine into the glass. He stared blankly at nothing in particular: a man in his forties, with refined features, though much wine had given him a slack and slightly uncomprehending look.

Laughter and conversation filtered through the window. Cho Ling drained his glass in a single gulp and moved to refill it. Then he was distracted by something unusual, a reflection that should not have been there, glinting among the bamboo canes in the fuel pile by the stove. He looked puzzled, and got to his feet, lumbering slowly across to investigate.

Under the cane a spiral-bound notebook had been awkwardly pushed in an attempt to conceal it in a house with few secret places. The slanting morning sun glinting off the wire had betrayed the hiding place. Cho Ling picked the book up carefully, and sat down in a wooden armchair near where he kept his spectacles. Minutely scrutinizing his find he recognized the handwriting of his daughter Ah Choi, just returned home after studying in the city.

He began to leaf through the pages. The book appeared to be her diary. Cho Ling loved his daughter and was soon absorbed, untroubled by any twinge of conscience. The neat script was more than a day-by-day record of names and events. It was an evocation of other times, times when life had been better.

It has been eleven months since graduation and still I wait for government placement. Part of me is so very anxious to know where I will work, where I will live. And yet part of me has never been so happy returning home with Father and Amah – returning to my own village.

He read on, his expression becoming tender, even compassionate, as Ah Choi poured out her most private thoughts, unaware of any audience:

Still I can't shake off the haunting questions of who am I, where am I going, what is my purpose . . .

He nodded in sympathy, his own thoughts miles away from the dim room, the table, the bottle, the untouched glass of wine.

Cho Ling's village was a cluster of houses along a single street. Almost all its inhabitants were workers in the rice fields or in the bamboo groves, spending their days toiling on the steep slopes that rose above their homes and merged with the mountain ranges whose cloud-topped peaks brooded all around. The city was a long way off, though modern roads and communications reduced the isolation.

For Ah Choi, returning home after graduation had been a mixture of great happiness and uneasy frustration. Happiness, because she was reunited with her father and grandmother; frustration, because her future was yet to be decided. Study had opened her mind to exciting new knowledge and possibilities, worlds remote from the secluded life of the village and the antiquated superstition of her grandmother, Amah the devout believer in God, longing for the divine miracle of which she had often spoken recently: a miracle, presumably, that was supposed to fill her frail body with life and health. But Ah Choi, whose duties included nursing Amah, knew that the miracle would never come. Scientifically and medically speaking, Amah's only future was faster and faster physical decline until her overworked heart finally stopped.

Ah Choi's studies had created no gulf between her and her old neighbours. Chinese revolutionary Marxism-Leninism placed labour and scholarship on the same level; university professors took their turn in the paddy fields each year. It was still the same Ah Choi who had come home, despite the fact that her city clothes were more contemporary than those of the villagers; and those who welcomed her had not changed either.

On her first morning home she had joined the crowd at the well, to draw the first of the day's buckets of water. Like most rural homes in China, Cho Ling's home did not possess a private water supply and the family's daily needs were met by heavy buckets laboriously carried home from the well. A crowd of villagers was already there,

waiting for their turn. Ah Choi was soon the centre of a
cheerful throng of villagers and excited domestic animals.

'How was it in the big city?'

'It was big!' she laughed. 'And there were many
people . . .'

'Your clothes are so *nice*', a friend said admiringly,
stroking the soft wool of Ah Choi's skirt and admiring
her crisp grey blouse. There was no jealousy in the comment. Ah Choi was back with people who loved her and
were glad to pick up the threads of friendship again.

Later, in the bamboo grove, she gathered cane for the
day's needs, carrying it in a small satchel. When she had
finished she began walking down the hill to the village.
She passed an old peasant woman struggling up the path
with a heavy load carried on an awkward wooden yoke.
Ah Choi helped her, straightening the yoke to make it
easier to carry. The woman's weatherbeaten, creased face
broke into a wide toothless grin of thanks. Ah Choi
watched her as she disappeared among the bamboo. *Is that
where it all ends up?* she thought suddenly, seeing herself,
old and bent, carrying bamboo on some future morning
years hence. As she came within sight of the village, she
was still frowning.

'Has the Preacher arrived?', demanded Amah, a thread of
spittle still hanging from her mouth as she tried to catch
her breath after another murderous bout of coughing. Ah
Choi shook her head, gently wiping Amah's hands where
the rice porridge had spilt.

'But have you heard when he is coming?', gasped
Amah.

'No, Amah . . . Now, drink.'

Looking after Amah was Ah Choi's main responsibility,
but was only one of the many duties she had. Life was
hard among the small community. Ah Choi as a young

and healthy daughter was expected to do her share of manual and menial work: carrying water, cooking rice, cleaning out the pig sty, turning out the bedding to air, and many other duties. It was a house with many crevices and few treasures. Most of the ornaments were cheap trinkets, gifts treasured because of the giver rather than their value, or souvenirs from visits to nearby towns. One family possession that Ah Choi treasured was a green singing finch that lived in a handsome bamboo cage, equipped with decorative porcelain feeding bowls. The beauty of its plumage and song had often cheered Ah Choi when depressed.

'He *will* come', Amah said. 'Today, tomorrow, he will come. And he will bring my miracle.'

'Drink', urged Ah Choi.

Amah grasped the flask and sipped greedily, but the exertion brought on another coughing fit. Amah spluttered so much that most of the water ended up on the floor. Ah Choi watched her helplessly, then mopped up what she could with a cloth. She hated seeing old people ill. Once Amah had been young, her skin had glowed; she had been able to run and leap, to walk long distances without help, to talk animatedly without coughing fits interrupting her.

Ah Choi wondered what it would have been like to have known her grandmother when she was a young woman. Even during her granddaughter's childhood, Amah had been a fit and healthy middle-aged woman. Now she was at the end of her life, and her body was giving up. All that fire and vitality, flickering out like dull ashes in a neglected hearth!

Amah's coughing was beginning again. Ah Choi held her hand, stroking her forehead gently.

The morning was wearing on. Out in the vegetable field

the Cadre was coughing too, the familiar disgusting retch
caused by incessant chain-smoking. Ah Choi shuddered
as she approached from the village with a load of mulberry
leaves in a carrier on her back. She disliked the Cadre.
The local officer of the Communist Part, he had prestige
and influence far beyond his unimpressive figure and weak
personal manner. Nobody knew what he said about the
villagers behind their backs, in the reports he sent to the
government. He was a man to be feared, and few trusted
him. Even his title, 'Cadre', emphasized his difference
from the other villagers: a military term in most countries,
in China a cadre – a *ganbu* – is an administrator, one who
does not work with his hands, a figure of authority who
tells other people what to do. It was a role that this Cadre
relished.

Ah Choi's father was with him, stooped over cabbage
seedlings, while the Cadre squatted by his side, his well-
cared-for clothes immaculate and unsoiled by work. They
were exchanging jokes, creating an illusory camaraderie
fragile enough to be broken immediately, should something be said to upset the Cadre. It was in Cho Ling's
interests to keep on his good side. The Cadre had known
the family well for years. He liked and respected Amah
and tolerated her religious fervour, laughing it off as the
hobby of an old woman. And since Ah Choi's return from
university, he had let it be known discreetly to Cho Ling
that he wanted to marry her. It was going to be difficult
to break it to him that Ah Choi had received that news
with hilarious contempt.

'It's nearly lunch time, Father.'

'Little Bird!' Cho Ling greeted her happily, using the
pet name by which he had called her since she was a baby.
'How is Grandmother today?'

'Worse, I'm afraid. She's still insisting that the Preacher
is going to come and work some sort of miracle.'

Cho Ling smiled tolerantly. 'Well, they are old friends. Maybe he will come.' At his side the Cadre scowled and coughed in disapproval. Cho Ling winked at his daughter. 'If our beloved Cadre can be persuaded to turn his back on such a meeting . . .'

The Cadre grunted with annoyance. 'That man would only fill her mind with useless superstition.'

'I can't argue with that,' said Cho Ling good-humouredly.

The Cadre pressed on aggressively. 'What the old woman needs is modern medicine.' He looked at Ah Choi with an expression half greedy, half shy: 'If you could only make your lovely daughter see reason, Choi Ling. After our wedding Amah could live with us.' He raised his voice to make sure that all the labourers could hear him. 'I am the most influential man in this village. Soon I will receive my own colour television set. I could see that her grandmother had the best medical care our district could provide.'

He sucked on his cigarette and grinned. 'All *you* need to do, Cho Ling, is make your daughter see reason.' It was as if Ah Choi was not there, as if he was trying to close a business deal. Ah Choi cut in to the conversation.

'His daughter has a mind of her own, thank you very much!' A smile took the edge from the comment but there was a steely quality to her voice. The smile continued as she added gravely: 'And, though she considers the Cadre a good friend of the family, she would prefer somebody younger.' She paused briefly, then decided to risk a further jibe. 'And somebody whose ego is not so . . . well-fed.'

The labourers within earshot giggled pleasurably at the Cadre's embarrassment. Cho Ling tactfully looked away. Ah Choi wondered whether she had gone too far; perhaps her father or Amah would have to pay the price for her witticism.

The Cadre's face showed how severely his pride had been dented by her mocking rejection of his overtures. Most women would have given anything to have a man of his wealth and importance take an interest in them. His composure thoroughly unsettled, he rounded on Cho Ling. 'You let her talk to her elders like that – in public?'

Cho Ling shrugged. 'My daughter has a mind of her own.'

Ah Choi turned and went back towards the village. 'Lunch will be ready soon!' she called back.

'You spoil her', complained the Cadre, puffing a cloud of smoke into the wind.

The accusation was regretful. Cho Ling's answer was similarly melancholy. 'Perhaps . . . But she is all I have . . .' His voice trailed away into silence as they both watched the slim figure of Ah Choi bearing its load of mulberry home.

'She is like her mother was', sighed the Cadre. 'Strong. Determined.'

'Bull-headed', agreed her father, and they both nodded sadly. 'She keeps insisting that she must love the man she marries.'

'Love!' snorted the Cadre. 'Is there no end to the Western nonsense that infects our young people?'

Cho Ling was considering how best to answer that question when a commotion on the edge of the cabbage field rescued him from having to answer it at all.

'He's here!'

'The Preacher – he's come back!'

A wiry good-looking Chinese a few years younger than Cho Ling was approaching, hot and perspiring; he had obviously travelled some way on foot. He had the sun behind him and the villagers were forced to shield their eyes against the glare, but shouts of delight soon filled the air as they recognized him and surrounded him. 'The Preacher's here!'

'Hello, my friends', said the Preacher, smiling at individuals and shaking the outstretched hands. 'Greetings . . . Hello! . . . Greetings . . .' The workers and their children had stopped work completely and were delightedly mobbing the newcomer.

The Cadre looked at Cho Ling. Cho Ling looked at the Cadre. Suddenly the Cadre burst into activity.

'Su Ming!' he exclaimed effusively, and strode over to one of the throng of villagers. 'Now tell me – about the problem you're having with Wang, your most favoured neighbour . . .' As he threw an arm protectively around Su Ming's shoulders, the villager looked nonplussed by the sudden attention. However, being a man with many grievances, he was not one to let a good opportunity go to waste. As the Cadre drew him away from the crowd round the Preacher, Su Ming was itemizing his complaints in full and enthusiastic detail.

Cho Ling watched them depart with some amusement. It was painfully obvious that the Cadre had opted to officially ignore the visit and was strategically quitting the scene.

'Cho Ling!'

The cynical smile faded as Cho Ling heard the Preacher call his name. He squinted from under his broad-brimmed hat at the younger man. There was an awkward pause.

'Is that you?' The Preacher sounded less certain, but his voice relaxed as Cho Ling straightened up. The two men examined each other with the knowledgeable appraisal of old acquaintants, but between them was also an indefinable strangeness, Cho Ling's manner in particular suddenly awkward and stiff.

'The years have been good to you, my friend', said the Preacher.

Cho Ling stood a moment in thought, then forced himself to a civil response. 'And to you . . .'

There was another awkward pause. The bystanders watched like spectators at a cockfight waiting for the first attack, the first raking claw. It was the Preacher who broke the silence. 'Amah. Is she ill?'

'She thinks you have come here to do a miracle.' There was an edge of bitterness to Cho Ling's voice.

Another pause. The Preacher uttered a short, warm laugh. 'Perhaps I have . . .'

This time it was Cho Ling who broke the silence. 'You'll stay with us, of course. Share our food.'

The Preacher looked troubled. 'There's the deserted school outside the village. It will be safer.' He loosened his necktie and mopped the perspiration from his chest.

Cho Ling nodded, making only a token effort to hide his relief.

The Preacher scanned the crowd, identifying old friends, seeking out newcomers. When he saw the Cadre, huddled in conference with Su Ming, he tensed. 'That man. Over there.'

'Our Cadre?' Cho Ling's voice was measured. It was hard to tell what he was really thinking. 'He's OK.' There was another awkward silence.

Suddenly one of the children pushed forward. 'Preacher! Preacher! Did you bring presents?'

His mother scolded him, red-faced, and began to apologize to the visitor. But he beamed at the child. 'Yes, I have! And it's the greatest gift a man can offer.' He laid a hand affectionately on the boy's head, as if in blessing. 'Or a little boy, for that matter . . .'

The other children gathered round in excitement as he reached into his pack. 'Tell me now, who can read? How many readers do we have here?'

Children and adults who could barely write their names

reached eagerly for the pamphlets, but the Preacher smil-
ingly sought out the ones he knew could read. It was a
task he was used to. The readers would read to those who
could not. 'You must share', he said. 'Please – I have many
other villages.'

Some way from the crowd around the Preacher, Cho
Ling stood alone, watching impassively. The cabbage
seedlings lay untouched as the pamphlets were carried off
in triumph by the lucky recipients. The Preacher at the
centre of the commotion was smiling, hugging children
and greeting adults. It felt like a holiday on a day when
no holiday should have been.

Cho Ling watched, troubled, wondering where it was
all going to lead.

CHAPTER 2

The last of the day's light was fading behind the bamboo groves, and the lamps were being lit in the village homes.

Su Ming was scowling as he pottered about his kitchen. The Cadre had kept him talking in the field for an hour, endless nonsense about procedures and investigations and how Wang would have to give an account of his actions. Su Ming wasn't taken in for a moment. He knew perfectly well that it was all show, an excuse to avoid confrontation with the Preacher. There hadn't been the same willingness to listen when he'd gone to the Cadre's house with his grievances, had there? And how may times he had done that! Was there ever a man as abused and badly done by as he, Su Ming, was? Was there ever a clearer case for a local cadre to stir himself into action and do something useful to justify all that prestige and privilege?

Anyway, Su Ming grumbled to himself, he hadn't wanted to talk to the Cadre that afternoon at all. He was much more interested in the Preacher. There wasn't so much happening in the village that you could afford to miss a diversion like that. But by the time the Cadre had finally stopped talking, all the Preacher's booklets had been distributed and the little crowd had broken up.

Su Ming spat in disgust and stirred the rice-steamer savagely.

The Cadre was irritated too, sitting in solitary splendour in his home, surrounded by his trinkets and small luxuries.

It had suited him not to invite a public challenge to his authority. He had an uncomfortable feeling that if he had tried to break up the crowd that had gathered round the visitor and send the villagers back to work, he might have found it very difficult indeed to persuade them. Better to pretend to be away from the scene, on important local business. Lucky, really, that Su Ming had been near at hand: for a change, there was some advantage to be gained by listening to the old fool's grumbles.

The Cadre's brow wrinkled thoughtfully as he pondered what to do next. Without doubt, an itinerant preacher would be of the greatest interest to the authorities, and there was great merit to be gained from being the one to tell them. The Cadre was looking forward to reporting the visit. But he would not do so until he had extracted every possible benefit from the situation. Ah Choi's grandmother, for example, was desperate to see the Preacher. A little bending of rules on the Cadre's part might well improve his chances with Ah Choi . . .

He sighed. 'How long, Ah Choi?' he said out loud. 'How long before you forget all your Western dreams?'

He was prepared to wait. There was something different about Ah Choi since she had come back – an openness, a restlessness that made her more attractive to him then ever before. She seemed to be looking for something, as if there was something more meaningful than the village and its labours, something more profound than party dogma and historical dialectic. Even while denouncing her for her decadent Western interests, he wondered secretly whether she was on the track of something that might give even his comfortable existence point and meaning.

Maybe when she found it she would share it with him. At the very least, she would make a good wife – when she had had time to forget her independent attitude, and her insolence to those who were her superiors.

The old school building was some way from the main part of the village. It was never used now, and the villagers hardly ever went there. Parts of it were falling down, the gaping holes in the roof letting in rain and sun and various small animals that sought shade and shelter. Now it was sheltering the Preacher. It was not the sort of place where anybody would live out of choice, but it was discreet, and those who came to hear what he had to say would be able to do so in comparative safety.

Inside, the Preacher was finishing his evening meal: a bowl of cooked rice, with cabbage and fried duck. It was simple food but cooked with loving care, the green cabbage arranged in an artistic circle round the edge of the white rice. It had been brought by a villager who had appeared in the doorway, handed the bowl to the Preacher with a smile and departed without saying a word.

He'd recognized the woman from his previous visit: she had taken one of his leaflets that afternoon. She would be at the meeting that night, he was sure. He glanced around the simple room. Yes, it would do fine. There was space enough for all who would come. There were few chairs, and the old school benches had disappeared long ago. Only a wobbly table, too big to carry away, remained. It didn't matter. He had let it be known that tonight he would be preaching about Jesus Christ. He knew that many would be there. They would have sought him out even if he had not announced a meeting. He knew the spiritual hunger there was in this village.

The Preacher ran his thumb round the inside of the bowl and licked it, savouring the last shreds of food. Then he bowed his head and whispered a brief prayer of thanks before unrolling his bedding, a strip of woollen cloth that offered scant protection from the hardness of the earthen floor. With a grunt of satisfaction he stretched himself out and closed his eyes. He was a practised catnapper, able to snatch rest and refreshment from the briefest period of sleep. Soon it would be time for the meeting, but first he needed to rest after the long hours of walking to the village. His last thoughts as he drifted off to sleep were about Amah. Tomorrow he would go and see her.

In Cho Ling's tiny house the lamps cast pools of shadow into the corners of the room. Amah was distracted, her eyes flickering left and right as she searched about her, walking unsteadily on frail legs.

'My shawl. Where is my shawl?'

'Amah,' pleaded Ah Choi, close behind, carrying a hurricane lamp and her outdoor coat. 'Amah – '

'I must look my best for the meeting,' insisted her grandmother. Ah Choi reached out a hand helplessly and touched Amah's bent shoulders, stroking them through the rough red wool. 'You're wearing it, Amah,' she said gently. Amah turned, her face confused and troubled.

'I *know* that,' she said, and gave her a wistful reassuring smile. Ah Choi's heart ached. Amah was so tiny and frail, and so ill. How cruel to deceive her with hopes of miracles! University had taught her the foolishness of her grandmother's dogged faith in God, but who could teach her how to handle Amah's sorrow when the miracle, as it was bound to, failed to happen?

Her father grunted in exasperation. 'Amah,' he growled, 'you're supposed to be in bed, you are ill.' He wrenched open the door of a cupboard and seized a bottle of wine.

'It is a warm evening,' said Ah Choi firmly. 'I will keep her covered.' Cho Ling shook his head cynically and stalked into the kitchen in search of a glass. 'And the fresh air will do her good, too', she called after him.

Amah watched him go, her expression troubled. She was carrying her Bible, grasping it so hard that her knuckles were white. 'Tonight may be the miracle,' she whispered. 'You would not have me miss my miracle?'

Ah Choi smiled at Amah. 'No, of course we wouldn't', she said, adjusting her grandmother's shawl. 'There we are. Let's go.' Her father reappeared with his bottle and a glass. Ah Choi looked back at him as she helped Amah to the front doorway. 'You're sure you don't wish to to come, Father?'

'No . . . I've got more important things to do.' He looked down at the red wine splashing into the glass. His daughter stood for a moment trying to decipher his expression. He glared at her resentfully. Amah's voice interrupted quaveringly.

'Come, girl. We must not be late.'

'We'll be home soon, Father.' She put an arm protectively round the old woman. 'Don't worry about Amah . . .'

Father, framed in the doorway, was already lost in his own thoughts.

The courtyard, once elegant, was now derelict. The steps up to the gateway were overgrown and dangerous. Ah Choi guided Amah with a protective arm; she was unsteady on her feet, but determined to get to the meeting. They were part of a crowd of people, moving towards the old school building in a straggling line, the lamps they were carrying painting huge shadows on the trees along the pathway. There was an atmosphere of subdued excitement. Everybody spoke less loudly than usual. It was important not to draw attention to what was happening, and in particular not to make the Cadre consider taking official notice of what was going on. For the present it suited him to ignore the fact that the Preacher had begun to hold Christian meetings, because of his friendship with Cho Ling's family and because Christians were his hardest workers in the fields. But nobody knew how long that situation would continue, or indeed whether the Cadre had already sent his first reports to his superiors.

Inside the tumbledown schoolroom the first arrivals were already worshipping. Many Christians had come from outside the village, and there were several in the village who had responded to the Preacher's earlier visit. Usually they met for worship secretly, not deceiving anybody but not drawing attention to themselves, knowing that they existed as a village house church only because the Cadre chose not to inform the authorities. But tonight was different, an opportunity to relish teaching from a known and respected Bible teacher, somebody who might be used by God tonight as the instrument to answer all the prayers that had been prayed for the conversion of their unbelieving friends.

Those approaching abandoned their attempts at secrecy and increased their pace as they heard the joyful singing that was already ringing out in the old school. They entered in ones and twos and sat down, a shadowy mass of people. There were no hymnbooks but the Christians knew the words by heart. Ah Choi helped Amah to one of the chairs and sat her down. Amah began to sing with the others, a thin quavering voice that showed what an exertion walking had been. But her face was radiant.

The singing continued. Sometimes when one hymn was finished it would start again, so that the same hymn might be sung two or three times in succession. There was an exuberance but also a deep seriousness there. The atmosphere of worship was unmistakable and affected everybody, even those who were not believers.

Eventually the singing came to an end, not because those singing lacked enthusiasm to continue but because spontaneously people were beginning to pray aloud. Ah Choi had never heard anything like it. Men and women were praying with tears running down their cheeks, pleading with God for the salvation of people who were mentioned by name and offered up to God for his mercy. She was somewhat apprehensive that her own name might be mentioned, and was relieved when it was not, though she knew, looking at Amah's raptly devout expression as she prayed, that her grandmother was probably praying for her fervently.

There was grief and abject sorrow in the prayers. Many of those praying acknowledged their own lack of courage, some even their own lack of faith. They confessed to doubting God, to being angry at him. Secret grievances that nobody had suspected were announced to a crowded room and wept over. 'Your kingdom has not triumphed in this village and it is we who are to blame: we have failed you, Lord Jesus', said one woman, whose broken whisper was barely audible.

Ah Choi was moved, but at the same time she was observing the phenomenon with the detached perspective of an outsider. Of course it was all nonsense, outdated superstition. But clearly there was a mass excitement at work here, a manipulation of the emotions: she'd heard about it at university.

And yet the over-riding impression she was gaining of the proceedings in the old school that night was not one of either chaos or hysteria. There was a purposefulness about the passionate praying, a solemn dignity to the ecstatic singing. These were people who meant business, she realized, and knew exactly what they were there for.

After what seemed a very long time the Preacher rose to his feet. He stood at the simple table, a hurricane lamp at his side illuminating his face. Ah Choi studied him. She remembered him from his previous visit, but she had been

younger and had not taken much interest in the man who
was as obsessed with religion as her grandmother was.
She'd noticed the strained relationship between her father
and the visitor, but her father often found it difficult to
be friendly with strangers. Anyway, the Preacher had been
so busy visiting the few Christians in the village that he
had spent little time at Cho Ling's house, and she had
been too young to attend the meetings that usually went
on late into the night.

He began to speak. His subject, as always, was Jesus
Christ. He launched into his theme with enthusiasm.

'People say about Jesus Christ, "He was a good
teacher." Perhaps you have heard him compared to Confu-
cius, to the great moral instructors of the past. A man
who taught correct behaviour, an ethical code.' There
were some nods from his audience. Ah Choi remembered
her professor in Beijing, paying cursory tribute to the
Sermon on the Mount as a primitive socialism. Amah at
her side sniffed in disparagement. The preacher shook his
head vigorously. 'They are all *wrong!*' he declared.

A ripple of consternation ran through his listeners. He
smiled. 'They are wrong because they underestimate him
so greatly,' he said. 'Over and over again Jesus proved to
us that he was *more* than just a good teacher. There have
been many good teachers in the world, but there has only
ever been one Jesus Christ. And over and over again we
can see that he claimed to be the only son of God.'

The villager were silent, digesting what he had said.
'He did not merely offer a system of good behaviour. His
message was not just one of loving one's neighbour –
though if we are to do that well, we must look to Jesus
for help.' Su Ming, sitting in the front row, grimaced and
nodded.

'Jesus is not simply a dead moralist, a wise teacher from
the past,' continued the Preacher. 'If he were so, who

would follow him today? We have had many teachers since. But Jesus is unique . . . He is not dead, he is alive; wicked people killed him, but he rose from the grave; how many wise teachers do you know who have died and come to life again? Jesus did.'

A murmur of interest ran through his audience, and the Preacher carried on, his voice firm and authoritative, yet with the lift of excitement he always felt when he spoke about Jesus. 'Let me read to you,' he said, and opened the well-worn shabby Bible that had accompanied him on many journeys. ' "I am the way, the truth and the life; no man comes to the Father but through me . . . I have come that you might have life, and have it abundantly." ' He closed the book firmly and held it in both hands, gesturing with it to emphasize his point. 'No "good teacher" can make such statements; unless he is a liar who should be locked up in prison, or unless he is an egotist consumed by a wrong idea of his own importance – or unless he is exactly what he claims to be: the Son of God.'

Ah Choi's attention was distracted for a moment by a sudden gentle pressure. Tired out by the exertion of the evening and the lateness of the hour Amah had fallen asleep, her head resting on her granddaughter's shoulder. Her mouth hung slightly open, a faint rattling snore audible with each inhaled breath. Ah Choi smiled down at her, loving her; then turned back to listen to the Preacher.

'It is through Jesus that God is offering us wonderful life. It is a gift for all people. Anybody can receive it if they ask him for it in Jesus' name.'

Ah Choi was intrigued by what was happening. She had come to the meeting because Amah needed a companion, but she was becoming fascinated on her own account. Meticulously trained to see the foolishness of religion and long accustomed to dismissing the Christian faith of her grandmother as the superstition of an old woman, she found herself grappling with whole new possibilities. Her horizons were in danger of broadening in a way they had not done since she first sat in a university lecture room.

Her university had been the university of Beijing, a campus of drab buildings and dusty libraries charged with an excitement that made it a different world to the village in which she had grown up. In the mid-1970s the university had been a centre of the conflict surrounding the then Vice-Premier Deng Xiaoping. Deng had been the moderate opposing the hard line of China's ruling Gang of Four whose political rhetoric was displayed on hundreds of red-and-white wall posters festooning the city. For a heady summer the students had supported him with demonstrations, only to be crushed by violence in Tiananmen Square. At least a hundred people had been killed there, and Deng was, not for the first time, the victim of a Party purge. Those had been the final years of the Cultural Revolution and of Mao Zedong's life, and when Ah Choi became a student in Beijing fifteen years later, students still talked wistfully of those days when anything had seemed possible. But during her own student years the Square was stained with blood again. Deng, rehabilitated after the arrest of the Gang of Four, had risen in power but had also grown old. The man who had seemed the great hope of reform had become the inflexible elderly hardliner.

In May 1989, on the crest of the wave of the worldwide democracy movement that was to culminate in the end of Communism in Eastern Europe and the extraordinary happenings in the Soviet Union in the summer of 1991, two million people occupied Tiananmen Square again in peaceful demonstration. Television viewers all over the world watched as the students made their protest and erected a huge makeshift statue to liberty. Like the earlier demonstration, this too was brutally crushed by the authorities. It is thought that 2,000 to 3,000 students and others were killed in the Square when the People's Liberation Army put down the demonstration with tanks and guns.

The world was horrified, but in the villages and cities of China very little of the true facts of the tragedy were known. The tightly-controlled mass media ensured that a version of events in which the students were branded as troublemakers and anarchists was widely believed. A picture of an incredibly brave young man standing in solitary confrontation with a tank in Tiananmen Square was published all round the world, but Ah Choi's neighbours had never seen it. In fact her own knowledge of the incident was by chance: she had been running with others away from the baton-wielding squad, and had seen the brave gesture for herself.

Many of those sitting with her in the old school building believed that the government had been threatened by an evil plot, that those who had gathered in the Square had been bent on wrecking the country and plunging China into anarchy. Carefully selected pictures and the accounts of the troops recruited for their known loyalty to the regime emphasized the same message. But in Beijing, Ah Choi had returned to her studies haunted by what she had seen. Where she was conscious of a deep restless searching within her, in Tiananmen Square she had seen young people standing for something to which they were committed far more than she had ever been committed in her life. She envied them.

She had immersed herself in studying for her final examinations, and taught herself to repeat the ideological assertions of her teachers. Ideas should be examined, they told her, and exposed where necessary: religion's claims were fraudulent, opposed to the ideals of Marxism-Leninism, and easily refuted. She gave model answers in her final examinations and returned home a successful student.

Yet even in the village she could not shake off the memory of her fellow-students' brave defiance, nor the simple fact that since the massacre, hundreds of them were becoming Christians. In some cases whole dormitories had been converted at one time. Ah Choi became accustomed to finding that friends who had previously been cynical atheists were suddenly transformed into believers, with a whole new focus in their lives and a smiling joyfulness that was as compelling as it was perplexing.

She thought of those students as the Preacher spoke. His words, for all their lack of sophistication and oratory, seemed to possess a power and truthfulness that struck an answering chord inside her. Could the 'wonderful life' he was describing be the solution she'd sought for so long – the purpose that would give her life meaning, and satisfy the hunger she had felt for years? She was stuffed with intellectual learning, yet she was starving in her heart.

A stealthy movement in the shadows outside interrupted her reverie. The Cadre was standing with an open notebook in his hand, quietly writing down the name of each person in the room, occasionally sucking on the cigarette that hung from his lip.

His cool gaze flicked over Ah Choi. She shifted uneasily on her chair and tried to concentrate once more on the Preacher.

CHAPTER 3

'Confess!'

Cho Ling's face was contorted, covered in blood and swollen with bruises that were already blackening. His tormentors were skilled at their job; the torture had been going on for hours but Cho Ling was still conscious, able to feel each blow of the length of rubber hose expertly aimed at his face. The hose came crashing down again. Cho Ling's head jerked back with the impact, then sank in exhaustion. But another blow forced him back again, staring at the ceiling with rapidly-closing, purple-bruised eyes. Now a pit of blessed darkness and oblivion seemed to be opening up, and it would be the easiest thing in the world to slide into sleep and forgetfulness; away from the remorseless lashing of the hose, away from the glare of the naked light bulb above the Interrogator's head, away from the sneering, well-groomed face that with a single glance could halt or intensify the punishment.

'Confess!'

The Interrogator's demand produced another flurry of blows. Cho Ling felt consciousness ebbing away, but refused to succumb. It was important, desperately important, that he should stay conscious, though the reason for doing so had long since escaped him.

'No! Please – dear Jesus – No! . . . No! . . .' From the next room a woman's voice screamed in a long wavering howl of agony. Suddenly Cho Ling was fully conscious, aware of the throbbing of his face and the excruciating stabbing pain in his skull but taking no notice of it. A terrible fear clutched at him as he remembered who the woman was. She was his wife, being interrogated herself in her own private hell in the next room.

The Interrogator leered down at him, a bespectacled immaculate official looking more like a local government officer than a torturer. 'Your wife is responding quite favourably to our methods', he said. A thin smile spread slowly across his face.

From the next room the voice rose again in a wail of pure fear: 'What are you doing? No – No – No . . .'

Then silence.

The Interrogator contemplated Cho Ling thoughtfully, then signalled his assistant. The hose smashed down again across the bridge of his victim's nose. A few drops of Cho Ling's blood fell across the Interrogator's cheek and spattered his spectacles. He removed them, wiping his cheek fastidiously, and watched the punishment continue. Soon the room seemed full of Cho Ling's grunts of pain and the ceaseless thudding of the rubber hose, rising in crescendo until it seemed to fill the whole world.

The bedclothes slid back as Cho Ling sat bolt upright, drenched in perspiration. His face was still contorted, just as it had been in his nightmare. He passed a clammy hand over his forehead, half expecting it to be covered in blood.

The same nightmare: complete in every detail, just as it had been each time he had dreamed it over the past few months. He had come to dread sleep, hoping that the wine that fuddled his brain would lull his subconscious to sleep as well. But too often he had found himself back in the tiny room, bruised and bleeding under the merciless glare of the naked light bulb.

Half asleep, he sat for a moment regaining his bearings then threw off the bedclothes and got to his feet. Amah and Ah Choi were still out, their beds empty – probably they were somewhere listening to the Preacher. The newcomer had been in the village for three nights. He had held a meeting every night and Amah and Ah Choi had gone to them all.

He paced the narrow floors angrily. Outside, a lone dog whined fretfully. He looked through the window. The pale moon was painting the hills in silver. Out among the bamboo groves, in the old school, the Preacher was probably still at work and Ah Choi and Amah were with him. The thought made the blood run hotly to his cheeks.

Trembling and still sweating from his nightmare, Cho Ling knew he would not be able to sleep again. Pacing around the room he suddenly thought of the diary, concealed in the fuel pile. He retrieved it and sat at the table, listening carefully in case his daughter and Amah should return unexpectedly. Then he began to turn the neatly inscribed pages of the notebook, absorbed in the narrative.

All of my life Amah had spoken of the teachings of Christ. And all my life Father and I quietly indulged her. Surely in this day of Darwinism and scientific reasoning, such things could not be true. And yet, as the Preacher spoke, and as he read the Scriptures – Never had I felt such stirrings in my heart, never have I heard such words – and never have words carried such power.

He raised his eyes from the diary and let his gaze wander, unseeing, around the small room. Yes, there had been a change in Ah Choi; less obvious than the changes university had made in her, but seeming to have affected her far more deeply. She had begun to change, and it had begun when she took Amah to that meeting in the old school building.

Cho Ling shuddered. Old memories were beginning to stir; images were flooding unbidden into his mind, images that he had kept at bay for many years but which came at him at night unbidden.

He had not always been a morose man; the lines of sadness and bitterness had not been etched into his face until he was in his twenties. The Cultural Revolution had been a terrifying disintegration of much that had been stable in his life. Fanatical teenage revolutionaries hounded any counter-revolutionary tendency real or imagined; a peasant who accidentally damaged a picture of Mao and an intellectual known to receive a foreign magazine were equally liable to be physically attacked and publicly exposed to ridicule and humiliation. He and his wife had even worn the dunce's cap and been led through the streets, and his body bore scars even now from the beatings. Small wonder that the experience came back to haunt him, and the prospect of his daughter rebelling against the authorities in any way filled him with a mixture of pride and foreboding.

He read on, his brow furrowed. How he would have liked to have told his nightmares to his daughter, to have had her comfort him, to have heard her tell him that it was all right, finished, in the past! But he would never tell Ah Choi about the dreams. It was better that she should not know. There was too much bad family history tied up in those times, too many memories nobody should ever dig up and explore.

Cho Ling slapped the diary shut and put it back in its hiding place. Now the memories had been stirred there was no stopping them. He loved Ah Choi, his Little Bird. After his wife died, after the pain and guilt of the Cultural Revolution, Ah Choi was all that there was left. In her all his hopes and ambitions were invested. She was a symbol of a better China, where the young would not make the mistakes that the old had made. But as he thought it, he remembered the teenage thugs who had been Mao's task force in the Cultural Revolution, and he shuddered.

It hadn't been easy. She had been a bright child and showed definite promise. When Amah used to go on about religion to her, the girl could usually find a smiling refutation for her arguments, leaving the old woman silenced and troubled. It had always been obvious she was destined for university. But you couldn't go to university by merit alone. Strings had to be pulled, money had to change hands, there were arrogant officials who had to be flattered even while the words stuck in your throat. He'd done all that. He'd sat up late with the Cadre listening to those interminable lectures on social progress and the dialectic of history, even backed him up in a few village arguments. There had been other Party officials he'd crawled to as well. Ah Choi had earned her place at university, but Cho Ling had paid for it in scores of ways.

Of course he would never tell her, though she had probably guessed that something like that must have been needed. Sometimes, when he was alone with the Cadre, there would be the merest hint of a suggestion that perhaps it was now time for Ah Choi herself to contribute to the costs of her education – by marrying the Cadre. Whenever he spoke to her there was an underlying note of possessiveness. Cho Ling would have been worried, but he knew his daughter. If the Cadre thought he was going to step into the role of husband unasked, he would find that a very modern young girl was quite ready to rebuff him.

The life of the village went on as it always had done. It was Springtime, the rice-planting season. In fields flooded for the purpose, bullocks pulled wooden ploughs made as ploughs had been made for centuries and peasants trudged after them driving the animals on. Domestic tasks too had to be done, such as the daily washing of clothes in the tumbling waters of the river.

The Preacher stayed on in the village, conducting meetings, talking with those individuals who wanted to ask questions about Christianity, and counselling and advising people with problems of all kinds. He was in his middle years, wiry and tough from long days on the road, but he was clearly experiencing mental and physical stress. Sometimes he looked exhausted by evening, but he was always ready to put off sleep if anybody wanted to talk late.

He came to Cho Ling's house the day after his arrival to see Amah, and there was an emotional meeting between them. Cho Ling sat in another room during the visit, sipping a glass of wine and listening fretfully to the murmured conversation. Ah Choi brought tea for the Preacher and found him sitting holding Amah's hand, deep in prayer. Her grandmother was weeping, but her face was radiant. The Preacher's Bible lay open on the bed. Ah Choi put the tea down at his side and left the room quietly. Afterwards, tidying up at the end of the day, she found the tea left untouched.

She continued to attend the evening meetings regularly, at first to accompany Amah and then because she wanted to hear the Preacher for herself. Sometimes she walked with him as he went on his visits, deep in conversation as she plied him with questions. As her interest deepened, the Preacher brought study materials for her and often discussed them with her when he came to visit Amah.

She was struck by the changes she saw in those who were responding to his teaching. She saw a new love and joy in the faces of some of her neighbours, and there was something extraordinary in the way they received and treasured the teaching materials and Bibles. They handled them as if they were more precious than gold, and pored over them at every opportunity. How was it possible, she wondered, for such a change to be meaningful? Many of those now reading the Bible were people she knew to be complainers, men and women bearing burdens of anger from long-standing grievances that had never been resolved. Yet now, as she met with them at the village meeting-places and watched them working at their tasks, she knew something *had* changed. These people were not transformed, they were not unrecognizable; but it was as if something had picked them up and set them in a different direction. Ah Choi, who was a fair-minded young woman, accepted that it certainly added credibility to the Preacher's claims.

She found herself warming to him personally, responding to his friendly personality and also to some indefinable quality she detected in him – a certainty and assurance that gave him the poise and inner resources to handle the pointed questions with which she pressed him. Often she confronted him with the arguments she had been taught at university, pressing him to answer the logic of her textbooks: 'It says in this book that we have to find the mistakes in our system in order to direct our future. Because how else can we direct our future? Just by having faith?'

To that particular question the Preacher had given a simple reply, one that did not match the intellectual expertise of the textbook. 'If you read the Bible,' he said, 'you'll find it doesn't tell you much about your future on earth. But it tells you a great deal about your future in heaven.'

'Sometimes I feel I am being rude,' she reflected later, 'using my university training to stump and overwhelm such a simple man.' And it was true; her teachers had taught her to be merciless in analysing the weakness of counter-revolutionary argument, and she had become adept at identifying the logical flaws in Western decadent culture, its materialism and its illusory religions. It was clear that the Preacher had little if any formal training in the study of religion; he did not know any of the textbooks she had been reading, and she knew for a certainty that her professors at the university would have had no problem in dealing with his arguments.

But she had an uncomfortable feeling that far from being stumped, the Preacher had answers that made her questions almost irrelevant. He somehow confounded all her learning. Often he had no answers at all to the arguments with which she challenged him, but he radiated a peacefulness and joy that were themselves a disturbing and conclusive answer. In a curious way Ah Choi considered that those evenings at home sitting with Amah and the Preacher – Amah sitting up in bed, following along with the discussion in her frayed Bible – were some of the happiest evenings she had ever known.

One night, watching a group of cheerful villagers singing a hymn, she admitted to herself for the first time that her interest in the Preacher's message was more than intellectual curiosity and the pleasure of spending time in conversation with a warm and intelligent friend. What he said about Jesus was making her think. Her university studies had dealt with facts and theories. The Preacher's message was about a way of life, a relationship, about a God who actually loved his creatures.

'This man, like many of the others,' she wrote in her diary that night, 'has something for which I grow more thirsty every day. How I wish I had such faith!'

As she returned the book to its hiding place behind the cane pile, she realized she had taken a step forward in a new direction. Where it might lead, she did not know.

Of one thing she was certain, however, and when she thought about it, it worried her. During her discussions with the Preacher, strolling in the fields or sitting discreetly by the river, she was often aware of the Cadre observing them. He was plainly keeping a record of every date, place and time that she and the Preacher talked together. She shivered now when she saw him standing on the fringe of the meetings. For how much longer would his tolerance last? When would that neatly-written list of names and dates be presented to the authorities?

She did not mention her fears to Amah because she did not want to worry her. But she talked to her about the Preacher, asking questions about what he had been like when he first came, and how he had come to know her family. Amah was vague in her answers, and Ah Choi did not know whether it was because she was old and wandering, or because she was carefully concealing something. Eventually she stopped probing and talked only about the meetings and the books she was reading.

'You see, Amah,' she said carefully, not wanting to offend, 'it is hard for me to consider what the Preacher teaches. I have studied at the university, and I am used to pulling arguments to pieces.'

Amah's eyes twinkled. 'And which of his arguments will you pull to pieces first?'

She thought for a moment. 'He says that God offers eternal life. I think that is superstition. After all, our ancestors worshipped spirits, and it is not long since our people worshipped our ancestors. Everybody feels the need to worship. And everybody wants to think they will live for ever. Nobody wants to die.'

'You might feel differently if there was a wonderful new life waiting for you,' said Amah softly.

Wish-fulfilment, Ah Choi responded silently. Aloud, she made some comment or other and switched the conversation to other things.

She was taken aback, and even more worried, when the Preacher announced that he was intending to hold a baptismal service in the river as soon as possible. 'It is a simple Bible act,' he explained. 'It is a picture of what Jesus did for us when he died upon the cross. Just as he died and was buried, so the one who is baptized passes under the water and is raised up into a new life.' She frowned, and he realized that what was to him a wonderful image and a central part of his life was new and strange for her. He explained exactly what would happen. 'Each believer who wants to be baptized will stand with me in the river. I will ask them to make a simple confession of faith and trust in Jesus, and then I will lower them beneath the water and lift them up again.' He was matter-of-fact, as if such strange behaviour was the most normal thing in the world.

'So that is how you become a Christian? By being submerged in a river?'

'No, Ah Choi,' smiled the Preacher. 'You become a Christian by bowing before God and accepting with gratitude the fact that Jesus died for your sins.'

'Then what does baptism achieve?'

'It *achieves* nothing,' he said. 'It is a picture and it is an action. The action is one of obedience. In the Bible it is taken for granted that new believers will wish to obey their Lord in this way. And as people in this village turn to Jesus, they will want to do so in their turn. And that is why I shall hold a baptism service, just as I hold one in every village where I stay as long as I have stayed here.'

'It's madness,' said Ah Choi sharply. 'It will mean immediate action by the authorities. You know the rules about making converts.'

'Yes,' he replied sadly. 'I am afraid that it will cause trouble, though I am praying it may not. But we will do it, whatever happens.'

There was a steadfast bravery in his eyes that could not be dismissed as foolhardiness. He seemed like somebody who had resolved upon a dangerous path because there was no other.

Ah Choi wondered how long it would be before the Public Security Bureau finally made their move. The Chinese Communist Party's attitude to converts was well defined; Ah Choi was familiar with it and had even argued in its favour while a student. The Party officially supported freedom of religion, while industriously preaching the alternative Gospel of Marxism-Leninism – a crusade made easier by the fact that Christians were allowed neither to instruct children in the faith nor to make converts. It was hardly possible to imagine anything more provocative than a mass meeting of new converts, publicly submitting to Christian baptism. Ah Choi trembled involuntarily. The Preacher was risking terrible trouble. Were his faith and his ministry worth it?

Even as she framed the question in her mind she knew his answer.

The Cadre was troubled too – distinctly troubled. He'd known how it would be and he hadn't been wrong. The Preacher had brought trouble into the village. It had all been going so well until he came walking out of the sun, just as if he had some kind of right to be there. The Cadre regarded the village as his territory, and resented the Preacher's easy popularity. Himself, he'd had to work hard for what respect he had among his neighbours. He thought of the nights he had sat up late trying to explain political dogma to small groups, and compared the dull response then with the positive appetite they seemed to have for what the Preacher told them.

But he'd persevered over the years. Even the Preacher's previous visit hadn't rocked the boat too much, despite the fact that some had become converts and practised their Christianity in various low-key ways. So long as they kept it to themselves he wasn't too worried. A private religion was actually less of a threat than something like the ancient Taoist beliefs that governed many rural Chinese communities. Now there was superstition for you! He knew some villagers that had Taoist leaders who could have been African witch doctors, with their bizarre beliefs and customs. And how would a local Cadre look who had to admit to his bosses that superstition and credulity were running loose in a Marxist state village?

No, far better a few religious crazy people who muttered their prayers in the silences of their own homes. Even Ah Choi's mother, flagrantly defying the state ruling against teaching Christianity to the young – ask Ah Choi how often she'd had religion rammed down her throat when young! – was just a weak old woman, somebody you could humour. She didn't matter at all. In fact he was very fond of her. And anyway, the Christians worked. How they worked! They met every quota demanded of them and more. The village was well respected because of their output. He wasn't going to jeopardize that if he he could help it: he didn't want his best workers going off to prison.

But the Preacher – ah, that changed everything. Now there were flocks of villagers attending public religious services, taking religious instruction, singing Western religious songs, studying that Book. The wisdom of Mao Zedong could be carried in a squat little volume with red covers and few pages. Why did the Christian god need so many pages to explain himself? But it seemed to fascinate his neighbours.

The Cadre attended each evening meeting, but remained unmoved by the Preacher's words. He always hid himself in the shadows, concentrating on busily noting down all that happened and everybody who was present. During the proceedings he watched cynically, remaining cold and aloof during the prayers and unsmiling during the singing of the hymns.

There was much on his mind on these occasions, enough to distract him from ever listening properly to the Preacher's words. The chief of the Public Security Bureau in town was already leaning on him. The Preacher's earlier visit had not gone unnoticed, and there were those in the Bureau who felt that the Cadre had allowed matters to get out of hand then. The Cadre groaned. He was mentally juggling the competing priorities of maintaining face with the Public Security Bureau, protecting Amah from the consequences of her geriatric foolishness, doing just enough to satisfy the dictates of his bosses, and persuading Ah Choi that she should marry him.

Had somebody asked him whether he was in love with her, he would have thought the question irrelevant. It was a politically appropriate marriage, and one likely to find favour with city and village. The question of love did not enter into it. Love was a corrupt Western nonsense.

And yet, as he thought of Ah Choi and the clear uncompromising light in her eyes, he was moved. He really was growing very fond of her.

Another regular attender at the Preacher's meetings was Su Ming, the cantankerous villager whose grumpy unpleasantness was a byword among his neighbours. He knew the Cadre was present and was fairly sure that his own name was in the little book. He didn't care. He despised the Cadre, making use of him when he needed his goodwill and ignoring him at all other times.

Su Ming was a difficult man but his mind was not closed. He decided to give the Preacher a fair trial. So he listening carefully on the first evening and decided it was worth a second visit. The next evening he listened even more carefully. The things he was hearing were intriguing: the strange, demanding person Jesus Christ, who had made extraordinary claims and backed them up with miracles.

He set himself to learn as much as possible. When a small group gathered round the Preacher in the afternoon to ask him questions, he hovered nearby, listening carefully to all that was said. When some of the villagers began to study the Bible cassette tapes that the Preacher had brought with him, Su Ming found an excuse to be working nearby so that he could join in unobserved. As the days passed, he acquired considerable information about Christianity – a subject in which he had taken no interest and of which he had known virtually nothing before.

He was intelligent enough to recognize, however, that what the Preacher was teaching was not a matter of learning facts. Time after time in the evening meetings the message was emphasized: 'You must do something about this, this is not just for idle curiosity . . . You cannot approach God as if he were just another marvel . . . He does not want you to learn about him as if you were going to take an examination. He wants you to respond to him personally. What are you going to do with all these facts I am telling you?'

So Su Ming the grumbler, the discontented one, the man whom people avoided if they could, set himself to discover what God might want of him. He borrowed a Bible from the Preacher and began to read the Gospel of John. He argued one or two issues that he needed to clarify in his mind, and those with whom he argued were astonished at the restraint with which he discussed the matter. He even began to pray, talking to God in a somewhat embarrassed way, feeling rather foolish to be talking to somebody who might not after all be there; but he was prepared to act on the possibility that he might be. Su

Ming was not somebody to walk away from a problem, as his neighbours had sometimes discovered to their cost.

But Su Ming was beginning to change.

It was the hymns that Ah Choi liked particularly. She loved watching the faces of Amah and her neighbours as they sang in the service. The words had such conviction . . .

> Amazing grace! how sweet the sound
>   that saved a wretch like me;
> I once was lost, but now am found;
>   was blind, but now I see . . .
>
> The Lord has promised good to me,
>   his word my hope secures;
> he will my shield and portion be
>   as long as life endures.

Listening to the hope and faith in the voices of the singers, the hunger that gnawed at her spirit was temporarily eased.

One evening, the meeting over, the villagers were leaving the old school to go back to their homes, animated and chattering. Ah Choi was among them, guiding Amah down the steps with the help of another woman. She was deep in thought, reflecting on what the Preacher had said.

'Ah Choi!'

A figure stepped out in front of her from the shrubs that lined the path. She looked up in surprise, then lowered her eyes as she recognized the Cadre. He seemed embarrassed too, as he beckoned her. The gesture was disguised as if he wanted only Ah Choi to see it. She stopped. 'I am sorry, I must go,' she whispered to Amah. Her companion smiled and took Amah's arm. Ah Choi walked over to the Cadre. He looked around uneasily. Several of the villagers were watching.

'Ah Choi, you must listen to me. Listen very carefully.' He spoke in a low voice, with an odd note of panic. She met his eyes, thinking as she did so of the notebook in his pocket. How many of her friends' names were carefully written there, neatly recorded with the dates and times they had attended the Preacher's secret meetings?

She waited, her face betraying nothing.

'I know you find these meetings entertaining. Because of your education.' He spoke almost apologetically, as if enlisting her sympathy in the difficult task he had of countering ignorant credulity.

She responded sharply. 'Not necessarily.'

He looked at her in surprise. 'You believe such superstitions?'

Ah Choi stared at him blankly. 'What do you wish to say, Cadre?'

'The people from the Public Security Bureau – they suspect that the Preacher is here. The district leaders are very anxious to find him. He is a wanted man.'

She could not conceal her look of deep concern. The Cadre continued. 'They must arrest him before he holds a baptism service. I've remained vague about his activities, out of respect for your Grandmother. But I cannot hide the truth for ever.'

There was a clear note of warning in his voice.

'Thank you, Cadre.' Ah Choi's voice was bleak as she held his gaze. There was little doubt how the Public Security people had heard about the Preacher's presence in the village. She turned to go home. The Cadre seized her arm, not ungently. 'My position cannot withstand such inconsistency.'

She looked down at her arm, hurting in the Cadre's grasp. He released her. 'I understand.' The Cadre was not even a bad man, she reflected. Just compromised, like so many. She rubbed her arm thoughtfully.

'It is not me,' he added urgently. 'You must understand. Those who follow the Preacher – it will not go well for them either.'

Ah Choi looked at him, comprehending. The implicit warning was unmistakable. As she continued on her way, her mind was in turmoil. The Cadre glowered after her, and sighed deeply in frustration.

Cho Ling was sitting at his table, a bottle and glass in front of him. He was gazing blankly into space, a comforting dullness spreading through his body as the wine worked its dependable magic. The terrible nightmares seemed unimportant when he was drinking wine and the troublesome thoughts that persisted in his brain had diminished to the level of pinpricks. Even the fact that there was no sign of either Ah Choi or his supper seemed of little consequence. Wine was a good friend.

The door opened. Ah Choi came in, helping Amah. Cho Ling growled. 'You are late.'

'I'm sorry,' she ventured, extinguishing the lantern. 'I was at the meeting.' Amah shuffled off to bed, clutching her Bible, distressed by the tension. There had been too much tension in the house recently. Her granddaughter made to follow her, anxious to make sure she did not fall. Cho Ling interrupted her brusquely. 'You know how I hate waiting for my supper.'

Ah Choi, her mind distracted by Amah's needs and still preoccupied with the encounter with the Cadre, pointed to the stove. 'It is here, on the stove, Father. You could have helped yourself.' She was annoyed and her resentment was apparent in her injured tone.

As her father raised his eyebrows in eloquent disbelief she bit her lip, appalled at the lack of respect she had shown. No amount of university training would ever remove the deep sense of courtesy that she habitually showed to her father. To speak in such a way was something that no parent with any concern for traditional upbringing would tolerate. Neither the atrocities of the Cultural Revolution when children were encouraged by the authorities to betray their parents for anti-revolutionary activities, nor the modern anti-traditional mood in the university, had completely erased centuries of filial respect.

Father, his voice dangerously edged, had barely uttered an incredulous 'What did you say?' before Ah Choi was already apologizing.

'I am sorry. It will not happen again.'

Father grunted. Ah Choi began to serve her father's meal. She felt no resentment, only shame that for a brief moment, distracted by the Cadre's persistence, she had forgotten her place as her father's daughter.

Three days later, she was sitting at the desk at home, absorbed in the books and pamphlets that the Preacher had left her. In the fields above the village she could hear the distant voices of the peasants chattering at their work, planting rice, cutting bamboo, or driving animals. No doubt the Cadre was up there too, watching and observing.

By the desk the finch was chattering gently in its bamboo cage. Amah was asleep in her bed, her breathing shallow and whispery, the frail regular rise and fall of her chest like the breathing of a paper statue. As Ah Choi turned the page there was a commotion in the street outside. Puzzled, she got to her feet and went to investigate.

In the kitchen she found Cho Ling, standing guiltily as if caught in the middle of some criminal activity, though Ah Choi could not see that he was doing anything to cause such embarrassment. She was surprised to see him home at all: he was wearing his work clothes, with his straw hat to keep the sun from his head in the fields, which was where she had thought he was. Nobody would stop work to make the journey back home from the fields unless they had a good reason.

'Father – what brings you home?'

Cho Ling's reaction was one of pure guilt. He fumbled for an answer. 'I came back for more tea, yes, more tea . . .' He indicated his Thermos vaguely, not looking at her. 'It's hot out there, it gets thirsty . . .'

He faltered, and Ah Choi in her turn was embarrassed. What was making her father behave like this? He began to stutter further explanations, but he was clearly telling lies. Then renewed noise outside rescued him; both stepped to the door to see what was going on.

Outside the house, an expensive black car was pulling up. The arrival of such a vehicle was a major event in the village; it was the kind of car that most government officials were entitled to, and they were always chauffeur-driven. Whoever was coming to see Cho Ling, it was somebody extremely important. As the engine came smoothly to rest, the village children clustered round the car, peering through the windows and pointing at the finery inside, as excited as they had been when the Preacher had come.

The car doors opened. Two men climbed out. One was a pleasant looking man of her father's age whom Ah Choi had never seen before. The other was the Cadre.

The Cadre was polite to the point of obsequiousness. He spoke to Cho Ling, barely acknowledging Ah Choi's presence. 'Cho Ling – may we visit for a moment?'

Cho Ling inclined his head courteously. 'Certainly. I would be most honoured.' The visitors moved into the house. Ah Choi followed. It all seemed very suspicious.

The two men were like actors in a charade, enacting a pantomime for her benefit. Her father and the Cadre were well acquainted; so why this sudden formality, and a visit that did not seem entirely unexpected by Father?

She did not have to wait very long. Soon introductions were being made, with that same appearance of a pantomime, a rehearsed performance for the benefit of Ah Choi.

'This gentleman is the Pastor of the Three-Self Church in the city,' explained the Cadre. The Pastor gravely shook hands, smiling warmly. Cho Ling provided chairs, and the visitors sat down. Ah Choi made preparations to serve tea.

'Ah Choi is not long returned from her studies at the university,' her father said proudly. The Pastor smiled.

'It is a very different world out here in the village, is it not?'

Ah Choi smiled cautiously back. She was wondering where this strange stilted conversation was leading.

'My family and my friends are here,' she said politely. 'May I serve you tea?'

She busied herself freshening the tea while the men sat at the table. When she returned, they were looking at a piece of paper. The Cadre glanced up as she entered. 'Ah Choi; this man – does he look familiar to you?' There was a strange note to his voice which she could not identify. He pushed the paper towards her. She carefully set the teapot down and looked. It was a photograph of the Preacher.

She stood for a moment frozen in panic. The Pastor's voice broke in, calm and pleasant: 'Have you ever seen him?'

Ah Choi thought rapidly. She tried to deflect the question. 'Why is he of such concern?' she asked politely. 'Isn't he a Christian, just like you?'

There was an edge to her politeness that brought an

uneasy silence to the small group. Then the Pastor broke into a hearty laugh. The Cadre and Cho Ling laughed too, in undisguised relief.

'Oh, no, my girl! He is not in the least like me at all.' He was clearly amused by the suggestion. 'He is a criminal! Instead of joining the Three-Self Patriotic Movement, he travels round the Province spreading hatred and division.'

Ah Choi looked directly at her father. He was avoiding her gaze, looking with acute embarrassment in another direction. The Cadre, also somewhat strained, joined in with the Pastor's condemnation. 'And it's not just him. There are hundreds more like him, rejecting Beijing's supremacy, encouraging illegal house meetings . . .'

The Pastor cut in, continuing what was clearly a tirade for Ah Choi's benefit. Indeed, she was rapidly realizing what she had already suspected; the entire visit had been arranged for her benefit, a veiled warning and a naked attempt to frighten her off further contact with the Preacher.

'If such an itinerant preacher were ever to come to your village, he should be reported at once. You understand that, don't you?' Ah Choi remained silent. 'Such people bring nothing but hatred and division to the Body of Christ. Not only do they violate Scriptures by opposing the Government Church, but because they have no single, central interpretation of the Gospels, they create confusion – well, you can appreciate the continual stream of false doctrine and heresies they expound.'

'That's right,' interjected the Cadre.

'Why,' the Pastor declared, 'there's even one cult that claims that if you don't burst into tears every time you pray, you're not even saved!'

The Pastor and the Cadre laughed heartily at this sally. Father joined in, less enthusiastically. Ah Choi watched them unsmiling and tight-lipped.

'*What are you doing in my house?*'

Amah's voice was freezing with cold contempt. She was standing in the doorway, looking at the visitors with loathing. She was standing up, holding precariously on to the door frame, her frailty momentarily superceded by the force of her anger. Her usually wan cheeks were flushed with livid rage.

Cho Ling got to his feet. 'Amah – '

She ignored him. Her attention was fixed on the Pastor. '*Get out,*' she demanded. 'Get out, get out of my house.'

The Cadre attempted to pacify her. 'Amah, he is a pastor from the State Church.'

It was the wrong thing to say. She snapped back at him, her gaze still on the Pastor: 'I know who he is. He is a government spy . . . a puppet.' The Pastor seemed transfixed, petrified by this whirlwind attack.

'Now, Amah,' remonstrated Cho Ling. Ah Choi, worried that her grandmother was too weak for such stress, crossed the room to her. But Amah paid no attention to either of them. She stalked up to the Pastor and looked him full in the face.

'State Church!' She spat, disgustedly, on the floor. It was a gesture of supreme hatred and contempt. 'Whore of Babylon! You are the ones who spy and keep records.'

'Amah . . .' protested the Cadre.

The Pastor, recognizing that matters were out of control, began to get to his feet. This crazy old woman looked as if she meant business. He backed away as Amah advanced.

'You are the ones who betrayed us during the Revolution.'

'You see?' the Pastor said helplessly, moving farther away from her. 'You see the division they spread, the lack of forgiveness?'

'*I* forgive you,' she said. 'But what about God?' He

winced as she bore down on him. 'You are the ones who are responsible for our arrests, our tortures. *Murderers*!' Her words lashed the Pastor like whips.

'You see the hatred?' he demanded.

'Out!'

'I'm leaving.'

'Amah!' pleaded Father.

'*Get out of my house!*' She was resolute, like a marble pillar, her face graven with hatred like stone.

'Let this be an example for you, Ah Choi', the Pastor said severely, but his authority was gone; indeed, he looked a pathetic, almost comical figure as he continued to edge towards the door, his hands raised as if to ward off a blow.

'Out!' Amah repeated, her eyes gleaming dangerously.

'And you shall know them . . . by their fruits,' the Pastor quoted, but it was the last exhortation he was permitted. As Amah pressed towards him he turned and made for the door, followed closely by the Cadre. Father, torn between the fury of Amah and his desire to behave correctly as the host of the bizarre meeting, followed them into the night.

Ah Choi watched them go, her feelings a mixture of hilarity and anger. But as she turned round to congratulate Amah, she heard a sudden groan of pain as Amah collapsed. When she reached her she was unconscious on the floor, her face a deathly grey pallor that made Ah Choi's heart lurch with fear.

'Amah!' She tried to help her stand up, but Amah had expended too much energy in the confrontation. Cho Ling appeared at the door. 'I heard you call,' he muttered, and blanched as he saw Amah. Outside the car doors slammed shut and the vehicle drove away.

Ah Choi, crouched over Amah, could not bring herself to speak to her father. She was full of emotions she did not recognize towards him: shame, contempt, and even blame. *It was an outrage to bring them here,* she told herself as she and Father carried Amah back to her bed. *He knew how much she respects the Preacher. He knew how much the State Church must answer for in the tragedies of her life.* Even if she had known what to say to her father, she would have been unable to speak for the choking rage that was inside her.

Father stared at her, silent too, grappling with his own shame and guilt. It did not require the stony silence of his daughter to convince him. He had done a great wrong, and he knew it.

The black car purred along. Its chauffeur looked calmly ahead, keeping his mind on the road. In the back of the vehicle the Three-Self Pastor sat trembling.

He hated scenes. There was something profoundly unedifying about them. Even though he had been wholly in the right, it was not good to be abused by an elderly woman, especially one so deluded by unscrupulous false teachers.

Of course the Preacher was in the area. He knew perfectly well that Ah Choi had recognized the picture. She had not been able to conceal the flash of recognition. And he had been in the house. Cho Ling had said as much, though carefully avoiding an outright statement. The Cadre had not been so reluctant to accuse. Lord, how he disliked that man! But dealing with the Cadre and pretending to be impressed with him was part of the job.

It was quite imcomprehensible that the villagers should refuse to be part of his fellowship. After so many years of obscurity the churches were open again. In the cities people went openly to worship now. He thought back upon his own experiences, how he had been a child when the Japanese invaded: his parents were churchgoers, and they were beaten up regularly. But a couple who'd come to China from Singapore spent hours with them, counselling them and encouraging them, and by the time the Japanese had been kicked out the little fellowship of believers his parents had established had grown and flourished.

They'd met in secret for worship, in each other's houses, of course they had. But once the Japanese had gone they came back into public life. And now it was like that again. The Cultural Revolution was long over, and the government had established a Church to which all Chinese Protestants could belong.

So why did Amah and her friends not join? Could they not see that it was better to be united, that denominations were an abomination to God? Of course it was necessary to compromise. Everybody knew that the Communists had a big hand in running the Three-Self Church. He was a Party member himself. But his loyalty was to God. If it came to a crisis, he would stand for what he believed. Party membership was only a piece of paper. It wasn't like the old days, when you had to bow down and worship Mao Zedong.

The Pastor was a good man but weak. He practised his religion sincerely, and he would not deny that moment in his life when, as a teenager, he had committed his future to God and believed in Jesus. That was why he was a pastor today, he told himself. When he preached, even Party officials sometimes came to listen!

But those stupid people in Cho Ling's village were on a collision course with disaster. They refused to compromise. By so doing they were bringing the Church of Christ into disgrace and putting the welfare of their neighbours at risk. He had no choice. As a responsible pastor and citizen, he must place the whole matter in the hands of the Public Security Bureau.

The realization appalled him. He buried his face in his hands. *O God*, he groaned, *help me do what is right! Help me have the courage to do this!.*

A few days later he went to the Security Bureau and told them his story, and was profoundly relieved when they told him that they could do nothing unless the Cadre filed a report.

Ah Choi, tired out by the events of the day, was sitting at Amah's bedside dozing.

The blanket fell back as Amah's hand reached out towards Ah Choi and tremblingly stroked her face. She opened her eyes. Amah's voice, papery and frail, whispered her name. A tender smile flickered on Amah's lips. Ah Choi grasped her hand gently and kissed it several times, cherishing it as if it were a piece of precious porcelain, too fragile to be put down with the greatest care.

Some sixth sense made her look up sharply at her grandmother's face. With a dull shock, she saw that Amah's exhausted features were oddly slack, and the almost imperceptible breathing had ceased. There was a strange absence to her body, as if Amah was no longer inhabiting it. So this was it: the moment Ah Choi had been expecting and fearing for so long, as she had seen Amah's indomitable spirit fighting harder and harder against the imprisoning, fragile body that was so sick.

She was still holding Amah's lifeless hand. She grasped it more tightly in both her own, caressing it, making it stroke her face again. Tears trickled down her cheeks. She flung herself across her grandmother's lifeless body and buried her face, sobbing, in the blankets. Alone with Amah's body, she wept in silence.

CHAPTER 4

Father was asleep. He was dreaming, back in his own private hell; he had been there often, since Amah died.

It was all the same, just as it always had been – the chair to which he was bound, the smiling bespectacled Interrogator, the naked light bulb above his head. The bulb, just now, was slightly dimmer; from the adjoining room the crackle of electricity could be heard followed by an ominous sizzling sound. Through the open door a faint acrid smell was drifting. Cho Ling knew the smell. It was that of burning human flesh.

The screaming had begun in the next room, an echoing high-pitched scream, a howl of pain that eventually slid into hysterical laughter. There was something demonic about the pealing giggles, as if the woman who was screaming was watching her own suffering and was amused by it. Cho Ling shuddered in his chair. This time he had been beaten viciously, not with the calm almost scientific precision of previous interrogations but with a hail of blows delivered with manic fury. His face was a bruised mass, he head sunk on his chest.

As the screaming continued next door he began mumbling incoherently. The Interrogator stepped forward and seized Cho Ling's hair. Pulling his head up, he glared at the barely-conscious prisoner. 'What?'

Cho Ling mumbled something, and the Interrogator stooped impatiently to listen.

'Yes . . .' Cho Ling's voice trailed off.

'You confess that you are a counter-revolutionary? You deny your faith?'

'Yes, yes . . .' The swollen lips stung him as he tried to speak. The Interrogator snarled.

'But you deny your faith?'

The electric light dipped again as the screams started once more in the next room, and the stench of burning flesh, the crackling of the wires, and the unnerving, hellish laughter began.

'Yes . . . yes . . . yes . . .' gasped Cho Ling, and the demonic laughter seemed to fill the universe.

Whether it was a hallucination produced by the torture, or another part of the dream, Cho Ling could not tell; but now he was fit again, and strong, and the hammer he held in his hand was as light as a feather. He could raise it high above his head, so he did so; with his other hand he held an iron spike firmly in place, keeping it vertical as he struck it repeatedly with the hammer.

And then everything changed again, a lurching shift into another reality where the iron spike was all that mattered. It was being driven into a human hand, deeper and deeper with each blow, piercing the skin and dividing tissue and bone. Over the relentless crash of the hammer Cho Ling's screams sounded louder and louder, a bruising crescendo of pain. *How could that be*, demanded Cho Ling. Was he the hammerer or the hammered? The victim, or the executioner?

Then nothing could be heard but a louder cry still, a roar of pain that filled the sky: and Cho Ling seemed to be looking from a height, so that he saw not just the pierced hand but the arm, the shoulder, then the whole body of a man writhing in pain while men were nailing him to a cross. The man's head was bowed, perhaps beneath the weight of its crown of thorns. But as he watched, the man on the cross raised his eyes and looked full at him.

Cho Ling awoke with a roar, sitting bolt upright in bed. His clothes were crumpled and soaked in sweat. His face was still twisted with the pain he had been dreaming.

The Preacher took the risk of appearing at a public gathering to lead the simple funeral service. Such an act was not in itself illegal, but the sermon the Preacher had prepared would bring instant attention from any official who came to know of it.

Amah's last act of witness was that open celebration of her life of steadfast faithfulness. Many who grieved for her discovered in the Preacher's funeral message the reason for her characteristic radiance and extraordinary reserve of physical and spiritual strength. 'She was frail and sick,' he told them. 'But she was stronger than many of you. She could not dig a trench any more nor put a bullock to harness; walking was difficult; sometimes she cried because her pain was so severe.' His eyes, moist with emotion, nevertheless glowed with conviction. 'Yet she had power such as some of you could not imagine. She was a personal friend of the Son of God, and he would do anything for her, he loved her so much. He died for her . . .'

Some who were listening choked back tears as the Preacher went on. 'Her sins were forgiven, you know: and now she has gone to be with God, he sees nothing of the bad things she did like we all do. She is dressed now in a beautiful robe, and all God can see when he looks at her is the beauty and purity of his Son.'

He brushed his own tears away defiantly: he had known Amah a long time, and her loss was a great grief to him.

'And you know what she would want me to say right now? She would want me to say this. There is *nothing* that I can say about Amah that cannot be said of any of you, if you will love Jesus and live for him . . . Amah was a very special woman, and we all loved her. But she wants you to know, she is no more special to God than any other believer. He loves you all, just as he loves her. We commit her body to the ground today, but we entrust Amah to her Father who loves her.'

Among the mourners, Cho Ling stood staring ahead, his mind revolving many memories. Ah Choi stood with her arm round him, listening intently to the Preacher's extraordinary words.

They buried Amah in a quiet grave in a corner of the village cemetery, out in the foothills beyond the village where few people went and the purple hills around added a solemn beauty to the scene. It was a tranquil place, which seemed to reflect the serenity that Amah had always displayed when she spoke of her death. Ah Choi went there often. It was a good place to remember Amah, and to think about the many questions that the Preacher's visit had raised in her mind.

She was there one peaceful morning kneeling beside Amah's grave when she became aware of the Cadre standing behind her. For a few moments neither spoke. It was the Cadre who broke the silence.

'She was a good woman.' He spoke gently, with none of the hidden menace and coded warnings that usually made his conversations with Ah Choi threatening. She found herself reflecting, not for the first time, what a complex and contradictory person the Cadre was. She did not doubt that his respect, even affection, for Amah had been genuine.

She nodded without speaking. Together they stared at

the freshly turned earth and the few flowers that family and friends had placed there. After a long silence Ah Choi stood up.

'So much for miracles,' she said.

The Cadre nodded sadly. Then, abruptly: 'Public Security is coming.'

Ah Choi gasped. 'You told them?'

The Cadre avoided her eyes. 'They'll be here today, maybe tomorrow. Sometime soon.'

Ah Choi turned back toward the village.

'Where are you going?'

'I've got to warn the Preacher!'

The Cadre grabbed her roughly by the arm. 'You will tell him nothing!' His voice was shaking, and his fingers were digging mercilessly into the flesh of her arm. She looked down, grimacing in pain. He let her go and tried to continue more calmly. 'If they find we've warned him, that we've given him help, we'll lose all our privileges. They'll expel us from the Party.'

Ah Choi shrugged angrily and turned to leave. The Cadre stepped in her way, blocking her path.

'Listen to me! *Listen to me!*' He had seized her arm again, ignoring her gesture of pain. 'Your education that your father worked so hard for, all the back-door contracts he has cultivated . . . they will all be worthless. Your life will be nothing. You will never have anything!' His grip tightened. 'Your government placement? You will be assigned to spend the rest of your life planting rice in a backwater community like this village . . .' He was willing her to understand the enormity of the risk she was running. 'The good life will never be yours,' he ended helplessly.

She rounded on him angrily. 'The good life – that is your only concern. It is all that matters to you.'

'In the end,' he agreed, 'it's all that counts.' There was

no confidence in his voice, no pride. He acknowledged it as if it were a confession of failure.

'Is that what you believe?' demanded Ah Choi. 'No hopes, no dreams – just pleasure, just serving yourself, accumulating material possessions?'

'It is all we Chinese have left,' said the Cadre defensively, as if daring her to deny it.

'No,' said Ah Choi hotly. 'You have not seen what I have seen.' A sudden heartbreaking memory flashed across her mind, a picture of a great crowd gathered round an enormous makeshift statue. 'The students who gathered in Tiananmen Square. They had a dream, *they* had a cause; they had something to live for! They had something they could pour their lives into, something that they – '

'But those students are dead,' retorted the Cadre.

His words dropped like ice. The light in Ah Choi's eyes faded, and the excitement in her face dulled as the Cadre's brutal dismissal registered. 'Their dreaming brought them nothing but death,' he said. 'Their beliefs led only to slaughter.'

Ah Choi's head began to reel. The Cadre pursued his logic remorselessly, like a hunting dog fixing on its prey. 'There are no dreams. Not for us. There are no beliefs. There is only self. What is best for me, what is best for you, that is all that counts.'

Ah Choi broke away from him. He followed her, keeping step with her as he argued. She was struggling to keep her mental balance. She felt she was sinking into a whirlpool of ideas, the solid ground of her few certainties slipping dangerously away from underneath her. 'There *must* be something else. Something higher.'

The Cadre looked at her with something like sympathy. 'There are no miracles, Ah Choi,' he said deliberately. 'You said it yourself. Not for Amah, not for us. There is only self.' He shrugged defiantly. 'And the sooner you see that, the happier you'll be.'

'There has to be more,' faltered Ah Choi.

'Perhaps for others,' the Cadre responded sadly. 'But not for us.'

She was losing control, all her theories and hopes were disintegrating. The bright hopes of Tiananmen Square, the defiance of the students who had confronted the tanks and soldiers of the government, that cry that had rung out from the heart of Beijing – was it all meaningless, a dream that had no fulfilment? And the words of the Preacher, and the books she had been studying – what did they mean? Had Amah died with a false hope, her faith in God proved useless by the arguments of the local Party Cadre?

'An appointment to high office, a refrigerator perhaps,' the Cadre mused, 'perhaps some day a colour television . . . these are our dreams.'

'No!' shouted Ah Choi.

The Cadre continued remorselessly. 'Those are all we dare live for, all we dare hope for . . .'

'No – no! I will not listen!'

Unable to bear it any longer she tore herself away from the Cadre and plunged into the woods, running at top speed.

'Ah Choi! Ah Choi!' The Cadre stared after the running figure, full of foreboding.

Ah Choi found the Preacher where she had expected to find him, at the old school building. He was not alone. Since his appearance at the funeral people had been talking about him far outside the village, and now he was swamped by a growing stream of enquirers from all over the neighbouring region. A queue of people stood patiently in line outside the building, waiting for prayer, counselling and teaching. In the open space outside were several small groups. Some were absorbed in reading similar material to that which he had given Ah Choi. Others were sitting in a circle round a cassette player, listening to a study tape. The Preacher himself was with a group of several people, laying hands on an obviously sick man and praying over him with the others. He looked up as Ah Choi arrived breathless and frightened.

'The soldiers! They're coming!' Her eyes pleaded with the Preacher, but he remained where he was, holding the invalid's hand. He looked up slowly, his mind still with the invalid.

'I wondered when they would appear.' His voice was calm, as if he was receiving information about the time the next study group would be arriving. He nodded thanks to Ah Choi, then turned back to the small prayer group.

'You don't understand,' she protested. 'They are coming for you!'

'I do understand,' he said quietly. 'But how can I run away, when there is so much hunger? And tonight is the baptism service. People from all over the region will be coming to dedicate their lives to God.'

Ah Choi trembled, remembering what the Cadre had said. The authorities would not permit a public baptism to go unchallenged. Such a public demonstration of faith in Christ, such evidence of large-scale conversion to Christianity, was quite unacceptable to the regime. But the Preacher's calm resolve was unanswerable.

'I cannot let them down,' he said quietly. 'If I who am a leader and an example of Christ show weakness and cowardice when danger comes – how can I expect my flock to do otherwise themselves? I will leave tonight, after the baptism.' The needs of the small group seemed to be of more importance to him than the prospect of arrest.

'They are closing in now,' she said, raising her voice in

an attempt to make him take the situation seriously. He
looked back at her, a warning, troubled look, but it was
too late. The villagers had heard her, and were becoming
agitated. A sense of panic was spreading. The Preacher
tried to reassure them.

'Please, please! Everything is going to be fine. Please
return to your studies . . .' He stood up and beckoned to
Ah Choi. He led her to one side of the school building,
where the ground rose in a small hillock. She followed,
still trying to make him see sense. 'You don't understand
what the soldiers are capable of. I've seen them, with their
clubs, their hatred – ' Once again, the vision of Tiananmen
Square rose up unbidden, a vision that most of China
would never see; the state television and news agencies
had kept the truth well concealed from the villages and
the cities outside Beijing.

The Preacher shook his head. 'I have seen them too, Ah
Choi. And I have felt their hate – felt it across my back.'

The stupidity of it all exasperated her unbearable. 'And
for *that*, you still choose to stay?'

The Preacher did not reply for a moment, but looked
instead at the people gathered all around, their fears
momentarily lulled. They had returned to their studies,
and the subdued hubbub of activity was resumed. Ah
Choi looked at the scene with him.

'Look around you,' said the Preacher quietly. 'Tell me
what you see.'

'I see simple-minded peasants,' Ah Choi retorted,
'believing anything they are told to believe.'

'Perhaps . . . Let me tell you what *I* see.' He looked at
the scene below. 'I see men and women who, for the first
time in their lives, have made friends with God. And at
the same time, have made friends with themselves.' Not
far away, a middle-aged woman was arriving to join one
of the groups. Her face was wreathed in smiles, and the

members of the group welcomed her exuberantly. At Choi recognized her as a woman who had been rather a lonely person, with whom it was virtually impossible to make friends.

A strange excitement was growing in Ah Choi, a struggle between the cold unanswerable logic of the Cadre and the assured confident faith of the Preacher. It was so simple, it answered so many of the questions and hungers that had tormented her since her return from university. If only it were true!

'An interesting theory,' she ventured cautiously, and despised herself for her reserve. The Preacher smiled.

'Is Su Ming a theory?'

In the group below her she saw her neighbour, the local misery. Su Ming, who was notorious as the village moaner, the man who could be depended on to find something to complain of in any situation! It had been Su Ming's complaints that had proved a convenient excuse for the Cadre to avoid talking to the Preacher when he had arrived in the village. But now – 'Do you remember how he constantly complained? How he was always quarrelling? Look at him now . . .'

Below, Su Ming was sitting with his neighbour. They were studying the Bible together, discussing animatedly and laughing together.

'I see people beginning to work together,' the Preacher said. 'I see them sacrificing their own desires, giving their lives to one another.' He looked directly at Ah Choi. 'They have discovered something greater than themselves, Ah Choi. And it is changing them.'

Ah Choi smiled half cynically. 'And you are their great Revolutionist?'

He did not reply immediately, but knelt on the ground. Parting a clump of grass, he retrieved a bamboo satchel.

Pulling it open he showed it to Ah Choi. It was full of Christian literature, mainly Bibles.

'Not me, Ah Choi. These. These are what is causing the revolution.' He picked three Bibles out and weighed them in his hand. 'And it is not a revolution of politics. It is a revolution of the heart.'

Ah Choi suddenly remembered the Cadre's warnings. 'And for this revolution you are prepared to risk your life?'

The Preacher shook his head. 'No. I give my life to the Lord. And to the people he loves.'

'You are a fool,' she said sharply, then regretted her tone; it was not his fault that he had embraced a philosophy that could not succeed.

'Perhaps,' he replied mildly. 'But until you have tasted that love for yourself, you will never know.'

'But I have read your book,' she said defensively.

'You have only read it with your mind,' he replied gently. 'Not with your heart.'

There was a commotion below them. A villager had appeared, running from person to person in the small group. She was looking for somebody. Eventually she saw Ah Choi and immediately called up to her anxiously. 'Ah Choi! Your father has sent me! It is most urgent. You must come at once!'

Without waiting for her, she turned and started back for the village. Ah Choi ran down the hillock after her. The Preacher watched them go, a troubled look on his face. He carefully packed up the Bibles again, and concealed the satchel once more in the long grass.

Ah Choi arrived back at the village to find a scene of utter confusion. In the street outside her home two men in the uniform of Public Security officers were emptying the house of every piece of furniture and scrap of paper. The

Cadre was supervising the process. The heap of family belongings grew steadily. Ah Choi saw her most treasured possessions tossed carelessly on with the rest. Nearby a small fire was blazing. It was fuelled by the books and papers that the Preacher had left with her. They were burning fiercely.

It was a bitter humiliation, the kind of punishment reserved for public enemies, people who were a scandal in their communities. The circle of villagers watching the whole thing made the disgrace all the more acute. Men and women with whom she had worked happily in the bamboo groves now looked at her with contempt and embarrassment.

Cho Ling was standing to one side, a picture of misery, his body tense with suppressed anger. She rushed to his side. 'Father! Father! What are they doing?'

He did not reply, only stood mute watching the assault upon his home. He was furious, not only with his daughter whose association with the Preacher had brought this disgrace upon him, but also with the Cadre, who was directing the humiliation.

'Stop them! Somebody stop them!'

Her neighbours were standing watching, but nobody dared to help her. An old man, his face etched with the pain of many such experiences, looked away guiltily as she approached. Two women with whom she had had good relations turned aside when she turned towards them and pretended that they had not seen her. Su Ming, standing apart from the others, looked on, his expression unreadable. When he saw Ah Choi he flashed her a sympathetic look and a brief, commiserating smile. It was a dangerous gesture which would have been unpopular with the officials had any of them noticed. The Su Ming of a month ago would never have risked it.

The Cadre was watching too, his face a study in conflicting emotions. He was paying a heavy price for the approval this act would certainly bring him from the authorities. He avoided the accusing gaze of Cho Ling. Selling one's soul doesn't come cheap, he reflected bitterly. He doubted whether his uneasy relationship with Cho Ling could be easily mended after this day's work.

Ah Choi desperately appealed to him and to the high-ranking official from the city standing at his side. 'Stop them!' she demanded. 'Cadre, you must make them stop!'

The Cadre replied smoothly, his tone dry and formal. It was a performance, carefully staged for the benefit of the official. 'It has been reported that you are associating with a counter-revolutionary. That you are harbouring his propaganda.' He waved dismissively at the books and leaflets, now blazing in the fire. The man at his side, resplendent in neatly-pressed uniform and gold braid, watched approvingly. His gaze flicked across Ah Choi as if she did not exist.

One of the Public Security assistants approached the official, carrying another handful of books and papers. Horrified, Ah Choi recognized her grandmother's Bible and other Christian literature that Amah had been studying.

'Sir?' he said doubtfully.

'Those are Amah's!' She stormed up to him and seized his arm. 'Keep your hands off them!'

The assistant shook her off like an irritating insect. 'Sir – what about these?' He ignored her, looking to the officer for instructions. The official gave Ah Choi a measured look. She glared back. He turned to the Cadre, weighing the situation. 'That is up to the Cadre,' he said coolly, his manner profoundly bored. But his eyes did not leave the Cadre's face.

It was an obvious test of loyalties. Any show of sympathy now would be interpreted as disobedience to the

Party. In her anger Ah Choi almost felt compassion for him, caught as he was between his desire to impress his employers in the city, and the affection that, she did not doubt, he had genuinely had for Amah.

'You have no right. That was Amah's Bible. Her whole life was in that book.'

The Cadre, pressured on all sides, made his decision. 'Burn it,' he said.

The assistant tossed the books into the flames. Ah Choi sprang forward, vainly trying to retrieve them. The assistant seized her and wrested her away from the fire. She struggled and almost broke free, but eventually he managed to bring her under control.

Her father merely watched as the flames crackled and licked the books. As the pages browned and curled, Cho Ling continued to watch as his daughter struggled in her captor's grasp.

The officials left the house in upheaval, the furniture piled in the street and cupboards and storage boxes indoors upended, their contents strewn all over the floors. To make matters worse, a thunderstorm in the hills broke out shortly afterwards and brought driving rain. Trampling in the mud, sorting through the heaps of ashes, Ah Choi discovered her diary, tossed – hopefully unread – on the pile. Her thoughts and fears, her gradual change of attitude to the Preacher, had been recorded in the pages that were now sodden ashes in her hands, the spiral wire that had bound it now twisted and blackened. She dropped it with the rest and ground it under her foot, destroying any evidence that might remain. Nobody knew what skills the authorities possessed. Maybe they could even read private diaries that had become grey sheets of ash . . .

It took several hours to restore the house to some sort of order and dry off the soaked furniture. Some of their

possessions had been broken and Ah Choi tried to mend
them as best she could. Her pet finch's cage had mercifully
escaped damage, and it sat on its perch as she worked,
chattering anxiously.

She was exhausted by the time evening came. But at
last she was finished. As she put the final items back in
place Cho Ling sat at the table, the bottle of wine in its
usual place in front of him. It was already half empty.
Father had been drinking heavily.

'He was our friend!' exploded Ah Choi, the treachery
of the Cadre still rankling.

Father shrugged dully. 'He was only following orders,'
he said.

'You would defend his actions?' There was bitter scorn
in her voice. Cho Ling paused before replying slowly: '*His*
actions are not what is threatening us.'

She looked at him with hostility. Her father's blunt
rebuke was unmistakable. He continued, in a leaden, matter-of-fact voice. 'You spend time associating with an
enemy of our government. Such treatment should not
come as a surprise.'

Her father's fatalistic attitude and brutal lack of compassion should have stung her into a bitter response. But
inside her a kind of light was dawning, a glimmer of
understanding which began to make sense of the terrifying
events of the day.

She tried to communicate what she was feeling to Cho
Ling. 'Father . . . Father, I am starting to . . .' – she
groped for the words – 'to believe in something. For the
first time in my life, I am – '

Her father interrupted defensively, pushing his daughter's dawning excitement away. 'I don't want to hear about
that,' he said abruptly.

Ah Choi persisted. 'When I listen to the Preacher –

when I read the words of his book – something in me comes alive.'

'I really don't want – '

'It's as if I have been starving all these years, and suddenly somebody is giving me food that really – '

Father roared as if stung. 'I don't want to hear this!'

'But why, Father?' demanded Ah Choi. 'Why is this so difficult for you?' Her resentment boiled over. 'You've been against the Preacher, you've been opposed to what he says, from the moment that he first – '

Cho Ling turned on his daughter, his eyes full of pain and anger – an anger made the more extreme by the quantity of wine he had drunk. 'Why?' he repeated unsteadily. 'Why? I'll tell you why.' He spat out the words. 'Your mother listened to those same words. She read that same book. And that . . . that is what killed her!'

For what seemed a long time there was a stunned, shocked silence. Cho Ling knew that he had said too much, that a secret he had been nursing for many years was now out in the open and could never be locked up again.

'What –?'

In his inebriation, Cho Ling still tried to repair the damage. 'Nothing. It was the wine speaking. You know how it has been today.'

'What do you mean – that is what killed her?'

Her father backed away, covering his face like a boxer trying to avoid a hail of blows. 'Nothing, Ah Choi – I meant nothing.'

'You always said she died from illness,' she accused him.

'She did,' Father said helplessly. 'She did, later on she did die of illness.'

He was looking out of the window, gazing into the distance and into the past – anywhere to avoid looking at his daughter. Ah Choi looked at him in anguish. Only his back was visible. He was a wall towering between her and the answers to a score of questions she had never imagined before.

'Father, talk to me.'

He remained motionless, silhouetted in the window against the last of the day's light.

'Father . . .'

Still he said nothing. She tried again, this time with a note of genuine tenderness; she was moved by his obvious distress which the alcohol could not soften. 'Please – '

There was a lengthy silence. Outside the house, the evening noises were giving way to night-time ones. The only noise inside was a muffled sob from Father.

Eventually he began to talk, slowly and with difficulty at first, his voice choked with emotion. 'Your mother – she was like you, so like you. She was always searching . . . always curious. Always the dreamer.'

Ah Choi waited without replying, afraid that the fragile thread of memory would be broken.

'We began to attend meetings,' he told her. 'We began to read the Bible.'

She was surprised but calm, betraying little of the emotion inside her. The principal landmarks of her life were being turned upside down; what had seemed certainties had all but disappeared. And in it all, there was a strange excitement growing in her heart. 'You became a believer with her?'

His lips framed a reply but the words refused to come. A soundless 'Yes' was all he could manage. Finally he continued, the words stumbling out: 'We began to help. We passed out pamphlets, held Bible studies. And then . . . then came the Cultural Revolution.'

Father and daughter shuddered at the words. Then unbidden images swam before Cho Ling's eyes: a naked light bulb, a smiling bespectacled face, and a voice in the next room that screamed and screamed. His face became contorted, as if he was being tortured.

'Like all Christians we were dragged through the streets.' It was painful even to think about it; for a long time now the wine had helped him to forget about the humiliation, the shame of public contempt. It was years since he had been forced to remember those days. Now he wanted to, he demanded his memory to recall the jeering crowds in their Mao tunics, waving the hated red book, gesturing obscenely at him and his wife as they were forced through the streets with labels tied to them branding them as running dogs, counter-revolutionaries, superstitious religious fools. 'We were forced to wear dunces' caps. The people taunted us. They made us ridiculous. Then later we were beaten and tortured.'

A cold hand of terror was gripping Ah Choi, but it was as nothing compared to the horror that her father was going through. The nightmare images and sounds were sharp and clear now. 'Things were done to us that may not be mentioned. They tried anything, any torture that might make us give up our faith.'

It was as if he was being tortured all over again, but this time in cold, waking reality, not in a drunken dream that would fade. The memories were almost too strong to be endured. He was forced to stop his narrative for a moment as he grappled with his emotion. When he began again tears were spilling on to his cheeks.

'Your mother . . . No matter what they did to her, she would not give in. No matter what they did to her body, no matter what they did to her mind . . .' He gulped back a sob.

His mind was back now in the nightmare, in a room with a bare light bulb, in which his wife was screaming. She was tied roughly in a chair, and the Interrogator was carefully attaching electrodes to her fingers. Once again he heard the sizzle of the volts burning her flesh, watched the Interrogator's nose fastidiously wrinkle as the acrid smell drifted across the room, heard the agony in her voice.

'She was stronger than I ever dreamed it was possible to be. A handful of them hung on. Your mother did. The Preacher did. They never denied their faith. But the rest of us . . .'

His voice trailed off. He was unable to continue, as the memory of his own betrayal and the strength of his remorse overwhelmed him. His tears were flowing freely now. Tears of sympathy were in Ah Choi's eyes too. She reached out for him, but changed her mind and drew back: for a grief like Cho Ling's, there could be no words of comfort, no consolation.

He turned to her, his wine glass forgotten in his hand. His remorse was slowly turning into anger. 'And you – don't you see? Don't you *see*? If you continue on this path, your fate will be the same as your mother's!'

She was unable to reply. His breath was rasping, his face livid. He was desperately willing her to see reason. 'Does your life mean so little that you would just throw it away?'

She stared at him, frightened by the strength of his anger.

He set the wine glass down on the table and confronted her. He looked massively strong and very angry. There was a bleak madness in his eyes. Ah Choi, rooted to the spot, was very afraid that he was going to hit her.

'Is that all the care you have for yourself? Is that all you care about *me*?' He glared at her. 'Answer me! *Answer me!*' The queer glowing fire in his eyes blazed as he raised his arm as if to strike. But he brought it down in a flailing gesture of frustration instead, hitting the glass and hurling it against the wall, where it smashed into pieces and left a red stain trickling slowly down the rough plaster.

Ah Choi's eyes, locked with his, were wide and frightened. The fury of his anger, his violence as he smashed the glass and the bewildering shock of the revelations he had presented her with concerning the past, were horrifying. Tears of pain and bewilderment started to her eyes.

Cho Ling stood trembling. His hands were shaking. In his daughter's terrified eyes he could see again the agonized look on his tortured wife's face. How much pain would all of them have to bear, before this thing had run its course?

He turned from side to side as if looking for an answer, then turned abruptly and left the house, pale and tightlipped. Ah Choi remained where she was. *The Preacher*, she thought. Pieces were beginning to fit into place like a giant jigsaw. The strange attitude of her father when the Preacher had come to the village first; the closeness between the Preacher and Amah; the resentment her father had always shown when she had become interested in Christianity.

What guilt must have tortured him as he struggled between the desire to protect and provide for his daughter, and the sense of betrayal that must have lived with him ever since he denied his faith! How the Preacher's words at Amah's funeral must have cut like a knife, and challenged him to the roots of his very existence! Her father had been living a lie, and the Preacher had exposed it – not by choice, but simply by preaching and teaching. And the bitter tragedy of it all was that her father had done it almost entirely for her. That was why he kept away from the believers in the village, why he had not attended the Preacher's house meetings . . .

The trickling wine had almost reached the floor. *That*

will have to be cleaned up, she thought mechanically, and moved numbly to pick up the fragments of glass.

In a secluded place on the river bank, dozens of villagers and local people were assembled. Far overhead a full moon cast a silvery glow over the rice fields and the distant hills, and on the river the reflections of a hundred lanterns danced on the waters.

The Preacher's strong voice rang out:

Then Jesus declared, 'I am the bread of life. He who comes to me will never go hungry, and he who believes in me will never be thirsty.'

He was standing waist deep in the water. The crowd on the river bank pressed as close as they could, the worn and creased faces of the peasants registering an earnest hope.

Two people were listening with particular intensity.

One was Cho Ling. He was standing apart from the others. He was worried that something was going to go terribly wrong, that his feelings of foreboding were about to be proved right. He was sober now, his face ravaged by the physical and spiritual stress of the past forty-eight hours. He was carefully listening to the Preacher's words, alert for anything provocative, not knowing what he could do anyway if the Preacher did bring the wrath of the authorities down upon him.

Also listening with rapt attention was Ah Choi, standing in the main crowd. The Preacher's quotations from the Bible were affecting her profoundly. How could words written so long ago have such an effect on her? But she knew what the Preacher would answer, for he had said it to her many times. 'This is not a dead book. It is a communication to living people, spoken by a living God.

And you must answer. He will not force you to be for him or against him, but respond to him you must.'

She gazed at the slight figure in the river, straining to catch every word, every inflection.

Over all, the moonlight and lanterns bathed the scene with an almost mystical glow as the Preacher repeated the words of Jesus.

But here is the bread that comes down from heaven, which a man may eat and not die. I am the living bread that came down from heaven. If a man eats of this bread, he will live for ever.

He came to the end of his sermon and closed his Bible. He looked at the people with a compassionate yet challenging expression. 'Who among you is willing to eat this bread? Who among you is willing to give his life to Jesus? Let him come forward now!'

There was a stir in the crowd as several peasants began to make their way into the water towards him. The Preacher's voice rose exultantly. 'Let him put to death his old life, and rise from these waters fresh and alive in Christ Jesus!'

The trickle of people became a stream, a tributary of individuals flowing into the wide river. The Preacher moved to receive them. A young woman, who had come forward with her husband, was the first to reach him. He took her hand. 'Kneel,' he said, and she did so as he spoke the words of baptism: 'I baptize you in the name of the Father, the Son and the Holy Spirit.' Then he gently lowered her into the water. Her face bore a look of sublime joy, exploding into a broad smile of happiness as she emerged from the water. She reached out and hugged a nearby family member, weeping with happiness. In the shadows Cho Ling watched impassively, his features giving no clue to his thoughts.

Ah Choi's thoughts were racing furiously. It was as if she were alone on the river bank, as if the crowd that pressed round her didn't exist. She was conscious only of herself and the unseen, almost tangible presence of God, and a sense of grave expectancy.

A queue formed around and past her, a straggling line of people stretching from the river bank to the deeper water where the Preacher was. One by one they went through the simple ritual, and soon the slowly moving line of believers out to the Preacher was matched by another of newly-baptized people moving back radiant with joy.

As he turned to receive the next candidate, the Preacher's face registered astonishment, pleasure and affection in rapid succession. Ah Choi was smiling gravely back at him, somewhat self-conscious as she waited in the waist-high waters. He took her hand, and prepared to baptize her. She waited for the now-familiar words of baptism.

But before he could speak them the night erupted in lights and noise. There was a roar of vehicles heading towards the river. The beams of their headlamps appeared through the bamboo before the vehicles themselves came into view: an official car, followed by two army trucks.

The vehicles braked sharply and soldiers emerged from the trucks, two dozen or more, carrying batons. They rapidly positioned themselves on the perimeter of the crowd, preventing anybody from leaving. The crowd began to panic.

A familiar figure stepped out of the car. The Cadre was revelling in his authority. He stood between the headlamps of a truck, on raised ground that gave him added authority. He addressed the crowd, assuming the air of authority that he enjoyed, though privately a worrying pulse of doubt was nagging at him. Perhaps this operation might not be so easy to control as he had thought. He launched into a reassuring speech, designed to restore calm, his hands raised in a calming gesture. 'My friends – please, there is nothing to worry about! Listen to me, please. You are in no danger. They will do nothing without my permission. This is only for your protection! Listen to me please . . . please . . .'

Gradually order was restored. The Cadre, his hands clasped officiously behind his back, continued his soothing words. 'Please. Our friends at Public Security are not interested in you . . . It is the subversive itinerant Preacher they are interested in.'

A murmur began to run through the crowd, and several people began to look towards the Preacher standing in the water with Ah Choi.

'If we turn the Preacher over to the Public Security officers, they have assured me that everything will be forgiven.' The muttering in the crowd swelled. The soldiers encircling the people stood immovable, their batons ready for use. 'There will be no fines,' urged the Cadre. 'There will be no penalties, your rations will not be affected.'

Arguments broke out all over the crowd. Some were tempted to do as the Cadre said, and edged towards the water; others moved to protect the Preacher, forming a human barrier. Voices were raised in anger as villagers shouted at each other, each attempting to silence the rival view. Everybody realized the seriousness of the situation. It would take very little for the army to move in, and their punishment was likely to be merciless. In his loneliness, Cho Ling remembered the long nights of beating and interrogation, and shivered in fear. Not many of the people gathered here were likely to get through the night unscathed.

The Cadre shouted, trying to be heard above the uproar. 'It is our only alternative! Please, they are only looking out for our safety!' But it was hopeless. Nobody was listening, and if they had been it would have been imposs-ible to have heard him over the tumult. 'Step aside and let them have him!' he cried. 'Listen to me! *Listen to me!*' But he was out of his depth and knew it.

Behind him, the bulky figure of the Public Security official stirred in the car. He emerged, dressed in full uniform; this was a wholly official army action. With an ominous look on his face he sauntered over to the Cadre and took up a position at his side. The Cadre threw him a despairing glance, but his superior merely shifted rest-lessly and looked angrily at the scene in front of him.

For Su Ming standing in the crowd it had been the most wonderful night of his life. He did not care about the chill that was settling on him as his clothes dried on his body.

What had he anticipated happening when he was ducked below the water? Even watching the joyous faces of those being baptized before him, he had no clear expectations, and so was not disappointed when he failed to experience a great mystical enlightenment or spiritual drama. Su Ming, who had lived his life grumbling and complaining, simply felt a sense of relief, as if a burden he had been carrying had been washed away in the troubled waters of the crowded river. When, days before, he had quietly sought out the Preacher and asked him to help him become a Christian, he had experienced a release from the oppression of years of anger; now, tonight, the process was complete. For the first time for many years, Su Ming was smiling even though nobody was watching him.

There had been much to be released from. He had spent

many hours in the past few days thinking about the past. He'd remembered the days of the Cultural Revolution: a young man with prospects, the future had looked good. Until a neighbour had denounced him to the revolutionary guards. He'd been accused of being a counter-revolutionary, of being revisionist, of having contacts in foreign countries. None of it was true. He'd even assured them he had no religious beliefs of any kind, so they couldn't attack him on that score.

But they hadn't needed a cast-iron case. His neighbour's lies were never checked. The guards, most of them younger than himself, had beaten him, daubed abuse on the walls of his apartment, dragged him in disgrace along the streets and dressed him in fool's clothes. Many who had been his friends joined in mocking him, out of fear of the authorities. What had been hardest to accept was the discovery after the revolution, that his neighbour had informed on him merely to gain favour with the authorities.

Ever since, Su Ming had lived as his own man, dependent on nobody, trusting nobody. He complained about anything and anybody: a child crying in the night, a woman taking too long a break in the fields; he had no patience and no sympathy. Complaining to the Cadre was a way of striking back. He was causing trouble for others in the way trouble had been caused for him years before – although, he used to remind himself bitterly, his neighbours would not suffer as he had suffered. And they were justly accused, whereas he had suffered because of somebody's lies.

Under the sympathetic counselling of the Preacher, all Su Ming's memories had been taken out, prayed over and then laid to rest. 'Jesus has made it possible for all sins to be forgiven,' the Preacher had said: 'Yours, your neighbour's, mine . . . everybody's. And if God has forgiven them, then you must not allow them to go on binding you.

Promise me you will throw away these memories. Don't keep them to brood over and make you bitter again.'

It was a different Su Ming who stood dripping in the crowd now. He was still his own man, still reserved and not easily befriended, but there was a gentleness in him that those who had known him long would find astonishing when they encountered it in the days to come.

But there was a fire in him too: a smouldering anger that this wonderful night had been interrupted. The scheming of the Cadre had succeeded. All the furtive note-taking, the posturing patronizing lectures, the pretence of concern for the general good of the people – it had all led to this: a gang of thugs with batons standing ready to attack a group of unarmed men and women.

There was a familiar tightness in his chest, the beginnings of black anger against the intruders and the Cadre who had brought them here. But this time it was different. With a dawning realization of just how different things were now, Su Ming bowed his head briefly and whispered a prayer.

It was like a blindfold being removed from his eyes. Suddenly he saw the soldiers not as mighty aggressors but as people like himself who had been frightened into obedience to the Party. The officials standing by the vehicles appeared tired middle-aged men hiding behind their uniforms. And the Cadre, swelling with importance but clearly terrified things were not going his way, seemed positively laughable. What power did these people have when compared to the Lord of the Universe, the Son of God who had died to save him, Su Ming, personally?

And so Su Ming, for the first time in his life, put his personal safety at risk for a cause he believed in. As the confusion raged around him, he suddenly began to sing, waveringly at first, then gaining confidence. He sang to those round him, beckoning them to join in.

Ah Choi recognized with a thrill the hymn that had been sung at the Preacher's secret meetings. As Su Ming sang, the crowd began to grow calm and then fell silent as his clear voice sang the familiar words.

> Amazing grace! how sweet the sound
>   that saved a wretch like me;
> I once was lost, but now am found;
>   was blind, but now I see.

Faith and peace were spreading throughout the crowd.

> 'Twas grace that taught my heart to fear,
>   and grace my fears relieved;
> How precious did that grace appear,
>   the hour I first believed.

The first to join in the singing was the young woman who had been baptized first. Another voice took up the hymn, then another and yet another. In the shadows, Cho Ling watched with amazement and the beginnings of shame. The soldiers did not know he was there. After a few moments of the singing he could bear it no longer and disappeared into the night.

The Cadre looked at the crowd in bewilderment. Su Ming of all people! Who would have thought it possible? There was something different about him, that was certain, and the Preacher had something to do with it. The Cadre gritted his teeth in frustration as Su Ming, still singing, turned towards the Preacher and marched towards him, plunging through the water until he was a few feet away. Then he turned his back on him, so that he was facing the soldiers again, and knelt down in the water. Others joined him. Those who had been standing near the Preacher knelt

with the others, and more from the bank pressed forward
to join the line of people kneeling up to their waists in the
river, facing their accusers with mute defiance.

The Public Security officer watched them, his lip curling
with contempt – a contempt that lingered as he shifted his
gaze to the Cadre. The people's purpose was obvious.
They were forming a human shield, a barrier of frail bodies
between the slender man, still standing with Ah Choi
where he had been baptizing, and the soldiers waiting with
their weapons. Soon the Preacher was almost hidden from
view, surrounded by his protectors.

'Stop it!' screamed the Cadre. 'What are you doing?
Don't be such fools! – '

But nobody was listening to the Cadre any more. The
voices were singing strongly now, and the joyful words
ran out gladly into the night.

> Though many dangers, toils and snares
>   I have already come:
> 'Tis grace that brought me safe thus far,
>   And grace will lead me home.

> The Lord has promised good to me,
>   his word my hope secures;
> he will my shield and portion be
>   as long as life endures.

The Public Security officer threw an ugly look at the
Cadre, whose unease was growing by the minute. He had
never expected such a challenge to his authority, his local
prestige carefully created over many months. Countless
conversations in which he had cunningly built relationships of treachery and deceit, seeking out those with
grudges and grievances – it was gone for nothing, meaningless in the face of the first test of loyalty.

He looked for faces in the crowd, people he had helped in the past, individuals who owed him favours in return. 'Wang . . . Lin Ho . . . You don't owe this man anything! They'll destroy you . . . You must stop, stop this nonsense at once . . .'

It was useless. Wang and Lin Ho were singing with the rest, their eyes on the soldiers. The Cadre watched helplessly, aware that he was confronting a phenomenon he did not understand and could not control any more. The Preacher too, temporarily safe behind his supporters, was astonished. He was dumbfounded, and was extremely uneasy about what was happening. When he had decided to hold the baptismal service, he had known that it was likely to place him in extreme danger. But the situation was a threat to the safety of the whole village. He watched the soldiers too, and tried to read the expressions of the Cadre and the Public Security officer, who was by now openly losing patience.

Ah Choi, at the Preacher's side, was astonished and excited by what was happening. This was that joy and faith she had been seeking, a faith that could move a handful of weak and helpless individuals to stand up to the ugly strength of the armed soldiers. These people were risking terrible consequences for Jesus, they were risking their lives for him!

The tension was swiftly resolved. The Public Security official barked an order to his troops. 'Stand ready!' His voice cut through the uproar; everybody heard it. The soldiers braced themselves for action, their batons readied in their hands.

The Cadre's dilemma was written plainly in his expression of pure panic. The people on the river bank were his fellow villagers, many of them friends. Yet he had his position to consider, a position that had been laboriously won. He hesitated, torn between loyalty to the people with whom he lived each day, and obedience to the government officials who maintained him in the privileged lifestyle that went with his job.

The peasants were still kneeling, still singing. The Security official was shouting to the Cadre, but what he was saying was inaudible because of the singing. But the message was clear, and the Cadre understood it. The official was not going to give the order to attack unless the Cadre gave his consent.

The Cadre was becoming desperate. For a few precious moments he resisted the pressure, knowing that one word from him would launch the full savagery of the soldiers' attack. The surging verses of the hymn were like waves threatening to engulf him; he felt giddy and light-headed. His face twisted in frustration as he wrestled with the crisis.

The officer was still shouting at him, a jagged scream cutting through the singing. The soldiers were standing in line, their batons poised. All they needed was his authority. As a local cadre he had spent long years trying to manoeuvre himself into just such a position as this. Now he had power and authority. If he gave the order, the soldiers would be sent into the crowd. In terms of his political career, it was a triumph. In terms of his self-respect as a person, in terms of the relationships he cared about, in terms of that respect for human dignity that he had never quite abandoned in his search for power, it was a disaster.

He lost the battle, just as he had lost many others, out of sheer exhaustion and an inability to decide what to do. There were simply no evasions left. He inclined his head in the briefest of nods, and groaned within himself. The officer, satisfied, wheeled round to face the soldiers and gave the order to attack.

It could never have been other than a one-sided fight. The villagers were unarmed and helpless before the advancing soldiers as they broke up the gathering. They marched, batons swinging, as if carrying out a training exercise. They had no pity for the very old or the very young and they beat women and children mercilessly. Anybody in the path of the advancing men was hit. Many received blows on the face and collapsed in agony. The soldiers marched on, trampling the fallen bodies beneath them, and entered the water to continue their assault, all the time getting nearer to the Preacher who was obviously their prime target. The Public Security official watched from the vantage point of his vehicle, a satisfied smile playing round his usually cruel lips. For a while he had been afraid that the Cadre would rebel, but in the end he had done exactly what was required of him.

And still the people sang. Out of lips caked in mud and blood, the words of the Christian hymns rose above the violence, above the cries of pain and the moans of the wounded. They held their ground as the soldiers advanced, and they were clubbed down where they stood. Those who were physically able stood firm, a barrier between the remorselessly efficient troops and the vulnerable figure of the Preacher, still up to his waist in water, watching in horror.

The Cadre was watching, too, aghast at what was happening. His mind was numbed by the realization that the carnage was happening by his consent. It was he who had given permission. Nobody else was to blame.

'Come! To the other side, quickly!'

Ah Choi pulled the Preacher's arm, urgently dragging him away. He responded as if woken from a trance, his eyes still fixed on the scene of violence on the bank. 'The people,' he protested. 'I cannot desert the people . . .'

'This is for you!' said Ah Choi, tugging him. 'Don't you understand? The people are doing it for you! Come on!'

Reluctantly, he allowed himself to be dragged into the deeper water of the river and out on the opposite bank.

The soldiers continued their work, crushing the small group as if maddened by the singing that still persisted, though many were unconscious or too badly beaten up to sing any more. Su Ming was one of the last to fall, bludgeoned across the face. He collapsed semi-conscious, blood pouring from a deep cut. As he fell his bruised lips were still trying to sing the hymn.

It was not long before the attackers realized that the Preacher had disappeared. Immediately, the Security officer detailed several soldiers to cross the river and hunt for the escapers. Others he directed to cut off possible flight through the bamboo groves and woods. A few were held back at the river bank to finish off the assault on the villagers.

Racing breathlessly through the trees, their wet clothes flapping clumsily, Ah Choi and the Preacher realized they were being followed. 'They are getting close,' gasped Ah Choi as they paused frantically for breath. They watched the light of electric torches bobbing along the path after them. Ah Choi put out her arm in warning. 'There are more of them ahead,' she whispered. 'We can't go that way. We'll have to double back.'

They ducked down out of sight and ran in a different direction. A clump of bushes crossed the path, and they flung themselves down behind them. Cautiously parting the branches, they saw three soldiers a few yards away, smoking and laughing together, guarding the track ahead.

'They haven't seen us,' said Ah Choi in relief.

'But we are trapped,' said the Preacher. 'They are on every side of us. Listen.' From every direction soldiers voices could be heard, and the sound of trampling feet as they examined every inch of the wood. They were searching every possible hiding place. It was only a matter of time before the two fugitives were discovered.

Very close to them there was a rustling of bushes. They shrank back as they realized somebody was pushing a way through the undergrowth. They froze. This was it; the end of their hopes of escape.

A man emerged from the bushes, stood up, and put his finger to his lips.

'Father!' cried Ah Choi. 'What – '

Cho Ling frowned. 'We must be quiet,' he whispered. 'Stay here. I will draw them away from you.'

'But Father, if they catch you . . .'

Again Cho Ling placed a cautious finger to his lips. '*If* they catch me . . .' he grinned. This was a new Father, one she had not seen for a long time. There was a conspiratorial smile on his face. Ah Choi found herself wondering when she had last seen him smile.

She began to protest, but he cut her short. 'I'll be fine,' he assured her. There was a babble of soldiers' argument, much nearer this time. Cho Ling took a deep breath and dashed off into the woods. As he vanished from sight a torch beam caught the back of his jacket, and they heard the soldiers shouting in triumph, 'There they are!'

Suddenly the woods were alive with noise and excitement as all the soldiers went in pursuit of Cho Ling, now only a distant movement in the night. Several of the soldiers passed within a few feet of Ah Choi and the Preacher's hiding place, but they were not discovered.

As the last soldiers disappeared from view, Ah Choi raised her head and watched them go. With a great sigh of relief she relaxed, listening to the noises of the wood returning to normal, as trampled undergrowth and broken branches settled back into place. A peaceful quietness

descended on the wood again, broken only by the shouts
of the soldiers in the far distance.

The Preacher got to his feet and made as if to go back
towards the village.

'Where are you going?' demanded Ah Choi.

'The Bibles and tapes. I must get them.'

'No!' Ah Choi was horrified. 'No, the soldiers will be
there.'

The Preacher, his face set, peered out of the bushes to
see if his way was clear. 'What other course do I have?'

'Run for it! Escape while you can!'

The Preacher shook his head. 'Other villages are waiting. They must have God's word.'

Ah Choi rose with him and stood pleading with him.
'They will arrest you, for sure.'

He was still carrying his Bible. He touched it. 'The
word of God, Ah Choi. This is the people's food. This is
all they have to sustain them. If I do not take it to the
villages, they will not survive. They will wither and die.'

He was implacable, determined to return to the one
place where the soldiers would look for him first. Ah Choi
let him go, deep in thought. But he had only walked a
few yards, still stiff and sore from cold and exertion, when
unable to contain the anger that was seething inside her
she blurted out: 'Is this how my mother perished?'

He stopped without turning round. Her angry tirade
was direct at his back. 'This stubborn blindness – is that
what killed her?'

He winced as if stabbed, unable to turn and look at her.
'Your mother was a great woman,' he said quietly.

Ah Choi struggled to keep back the tears that threatened
to overwhelm her. 'My mother died senselessly and in
vain!' she choked bitterly.

The Preacher turned round then, a great conviction shin-
ing in his eyes. 'Oh no, Ah Choi. You must *never* say

that. Your mother gave her life so that others might find life. *His* life, Ah Choi; abundant, overflowing life.' There was joy in his voice as he added: 'That is what we give. And that is why, if necessary, we die.'

The tears came then, from deep inside her, as the pent-up bitterness and confusion were released in grief that was mixed with a strange consolation. The Preacher placed a strong hand on her shoulder and sighed. Then, looking into the trees and undergrowth that lined the woodland track, he spoke gently to her.

'Look – up there. Do you see the bamboo?'

She raised her head. The leafy branches thrust into the sky, the moonlight barely penetrating the lush vegetation. She nodded sadly.

'That is us,' said the Preacher. 'The Body of Christ, we are like the bamboo. It makes no difference how fierce the storm is, how cold the winter. It makes no difference how often we are cut down. We always sprout again and come back. Not as individuals, but as a Body. And every time that Body rises, it rises stronger, more capable of giving life than ever before.'

'But if you die . . . How will those other villages be reached? How will the Bibles be distributed?'

'The Lord raises others up,' he assured her.

'But nobody has your training.'

'Training is necessary. But not as necessary as having the heart for the task . . . the Lord's heart.'

Ah Choi had many questions, but there was no time to ask them. Behind the two fugitives, a well-known voice spoke sharply.

'Arrest them.'

The Cadre was standing like a ramrod, his hands at his sides, his face like stone. He had several soldiers with him, and was standing on a small tussock of grass, adding – perhaps unintentionally – a few inches to his height and his authority. For a few moments they all looked at each other in silent confrontation. Ah Choi briefly considered running for safety, but realized there was no hope. The game was up: there was no escape. Everybody knew it.

The soldiers moved in, seizing the Preacher and Ah Choi. In the scuffle that followed Ah Choi, struggling to free herself, made a vain appeal to the Cadre trying to make him see reason. 'Let go! Cadre . . .'

But he ignored her pleas. 'Take them away,' he ordered.

'Let go of me! Preacher! Preacher!' But the Preacher was struggling too, held firmly in the grasp of another soldier. 'Cadre!' she cried again, trying to pull herself free.

'What about the girl?' asked her captor.

The Cadre looked through Ah Choi and past her, with no sign of recognition, as if she did not exist. 'What girl?' he responded. 'I can't see any girl.' He stepped down and walked off behind the Preacher and his captor, dragging uneasily on his cigarette.

The soldier holding Ah Choi nodded, understanding the Cadre's meaning. He contemplated her in disgust, and then released her with a gesture of contempt, almost flinging her to the ground, then followed the Cadre leaving her alone among the trees.

'Preacher! Cadre! . . . Cadre! Preacher!' But nobody was listening to Ah Choi. Soon her cries turned to quiet tears. She was on her own in the woods, cut off from her father and friends, with no idea what would happen to the Preacher.

As she stood weeping she saw a familiar object lying in the dirt. It was the Preacher's Bible, lying where it had fallen in the scuffle. She knelt down and picked it up, wiping her eyes. With great gentleness she opened it and began to read. Soon she was lost in thought.

She remained out of doors all that night, walking restlessly from place to place, often sitting to read by the bright moonlight, or pacing to and fro as she began to piece together the various experiences of the past week. When she had gone to university she had expected it to change her whole life; but it was in her home village, among people she had known all her life, that the change had come that threatened to turn upside down everything that she had ever regarded as certain.

She had seen heroism in the actions of the villagers that night and in the Preacher's fearless readiness to face the soldiers in order to retrieve his stock of literature. She had learned the truth about her mother's death; that she too had died in circumstances of the utmost bravery, refusing to give in to torture and abuse. Against the contemptible weakness of the Cadre, who had permitted most of his village to be brutally attacked, and the fragile, alcohol-bolstered efforts of her father, such acts of courage glowed like flames in the darkness.

Yet she knew that bravery was only a small part of what she had seen that night. There had been something else in the people's faces as they sang: a radiant joy and peace that Ah Choi recognized and longed for. Where had it come from? Her neighbours were not conspicuously brave nor particularly happy people, yet she had seen them valiant and transformed in the face of the soldiers.

Perhaps they are fools, she thought, and wondered how many of them even now were lying wounded in their homes, perhaps even dead. But then she remembered the quiet assurance of the Preacher, the hours he had spent in conversation with her and with Amah. And that parable of the bamboo, she thought; there was a wisdom there, a security in the knowledge that what the Preacher was talking about was a truth that surpassed all human truths. In the book she held in her hands, she recognized, was the answer she had hungered for; in the man Jesus Christ whom the Preacher had talked of was the person who could give it to her.

Through the long hours the peace and certainty, that had descended upon her at the river bank and made her join those wishing to be baptised, returned. As she read the Bible passages that the Preacher had shown her, she made up her mind. The Preacher had been taken captive, but he had shown her the way.

The first pink flush of dawn was glowing as Ah Choi returned to the river bank. She looked sadly at the evidence of the previous night's violence, the abandoned lanterns and Bibles trampled into the mud, remembering all that had happened there.

It has been a night full of sorrow and of knowledge, she reflected, *and yet there is still so much for me to learn. But I now know what I believe, and I know what I must do.* She stepped into the water, and waded waist-deep to the place where she had been standing with the Preacher when the soldiers had arrived.

There she baptized herself, murmuring the words the Preacher had used, remembering all that he had explained that baptism represented. She plunged beneath the cold water, and it seemed as though a burden was washed from her back; then she was rising from the waters, flinging her arms wide, laughing into the dawn sky, full of joy.

The night before, she had wondered what it would feel like when the Preacher baptized her. Now she knew. No fireworks, certainly; but a deep assurance was taking root in her heart. She knew that she had, for the first time, obeyed God, and that it was only the beginning of that new and wonderful life that the Preacher had spoken of. If she had had a mirror, she knew, she would have seen in her own face the same happiness she had seen in the people gathered last night.

She returned to the bank, oblivious of her soaking

clothes. It was still very early. She decided to go to the old school building where the Preacher had taught.

The stools and tables were scattered in forlorn confusion. Ah Choi wandered around the room, stroking their rough wooden surfaces, thinking how much had happened there. It was in that room that she had first begun to take the Preacher seriously. It was there that she had seen the transformed lives of Su Ming and the others, blossoming in a new vitality; the true revolution.

Then she remembered the hiding place among the long grass. She went up there and felt around in the leaves. The satchel was still where the Preacher had left it. As she pulled it out she felt its weight; it was full of Bibles and study tapes.

The village was asleep as Ah Choi came home, stiff and shivering from her night in wet clothes but heedless of the discomfort. As she approached her home she saw a light in the window, and she began to run, the satchel full of books bumping at her side as she went.

Cho Ling was sitting at the table, unshaven, his eyes deeply sunk in his face; he had not been to bed either. The bottle in front of him was almost empty. He was slumped in his chair, his mind numbed by the wine.

His daughter burst into the room, her face alight with happiness. 'Father! You're safe! I was so worried . . .' Some of the happiness faded from her eyes as she saw that he was already half-drunk. He barely registered the fact that his daughter had come home.

He patted her arm absently. She put the satchel on the table. 'They captured the Preacher.' Cho Ling's reaction was a slight movement of his head. 'These are his Bibles and his tapes.'

He stared at them woodenly, his mind too fuddled by the wine to take much interest. Ah Choi moved around

the room collecting a few belongings. She packed them
with some food into the satchel. 'I must take them to
Swatow while it is still early,' she said. 'The roads are still
empty at this time.'

Her father said nothing.

'Swatow, that's where he was going next,' she said
tersely. 'Maybe there'll be somebody there who will know
what to do with them.'

There was no answer. Cho Ling sat silent, his lack of
response an indictment in itself. Ah Choi sensed his anger
and tried to justify herself. 'I couldn't just let them sit and
rot, Father. Other believers need them.' She remembered
the Preacher's words; how strong they seemed now, how
vitally important! 'It is their food,' she said, 'their life.'

From a great distance, through a haze of wine, her father
finally spoke. 'And it has become yours.'

She went to him. 'Father, that is not true.' She meant it.
He said nothing. 'I will be back tomorrow,' she promised.
'Perhaps the next day.'

He shook his head. 'You will not be back.'

'What are you saying?'

Again he refused to reply, and stung into further justifi-
cation she began to argue with him, setting forth her
reasons for leaving. 'Father, I can not replace the Preacher.
I know so little about God. And the Bible; it's a wonderful
book, but I am not trained to preach from it.'

He would not be drawn into discussion. His silence was
more eloquent than any argument. Ah Choi continued.

'And miracles . . . everybody seems to believe in
miracles! The only thing I know about miracles is that
they do not happen. Look at Amah's "miracle". She never
received it.' In her agitation she did not look at her father,
but toyed nervously with a few ornaments that lay, still
out of place after the Cadre's search, on a shelf.

'No . . . no . . .'

Cho Ling's voice seemed to come from a great distance, from another time and place, a numbed, dull whisper. Ah Choi stopped speaking. 'Do you think Amah was praying to be healed?' he said. 'No. The miracle she wanted was for you to know God.'

'What?' In this night of consternation, another certainty was being taken away. As Cho Ling continued to speak, she could hardly believe what she was hearing.

'She wanted you to serve God, like your mother did.' His composure broke, and Ah Choi saw tears start to his eyes. Emotion made him stumble over his words. He could barely speak. 'Amah got her miracle. More so than she will ever know.'

'Father!' cried Ah Choi, and approached him gently; they were both distraught.

'More than she will ever know,' repeated Father, as Ah Choi knelt by his chair. He drank some wine defiantly and stared at the table top.

'I'm so sorry, so sorry,' sobbed Ah Choi.

He scrubbed his eyes dry with the sleeve of his sweatshirt and looked down at the young woman weeping by his side. How like her mother she was! The same headstrong determination, the same reckless commitment to do what was right regardless of the consequences. This one would get into trouble too, he reflected, and he felt a stirring of admiration not unmixed with envy.

The wine-fumes were clearing from his head. There were things to be done, matters to be arranged. His daughter needed his help, more than she had ever done so in her life before. If there was ever a time when she needed his strength and comfort it was now. He reached down to her with a dawning realization that he loved this headstrong girl more than anybody or anything in the world. 'Hush now,' he whispered. 'Hush, hush.'

'I'm so *sorry*,' she wept.

He laid a hand gently on her arm. 'Get up now,' he said. 'Get up and wash your face. Go on now. We have much to do.'

Ah Choi wiped her cheek with her hand and blinked the tears from her eyes. She looked at Cho Ling doubtfully, then with increasing understanding. A tremulous smile appeared on her face as she got to her feet and went to get ready.

He drained the last of the wine; his mind, now clear and resolves, was working hard. *It will not be easy,* he thought, *not for either of us. But if this is what she must do, then she must do it.* And he was determined to give her all the help in his power.

The sun was climbing in the sky when Cho Ling and Ah Choi stood at the door of their home to say their goodbyes. Villagers were already up and about, but the two in the doorway spoke in whispers, anxious not to be noticed.

'Be careful, little one,' murmured Ah Choi. Without thinking, he adjusted her scarf and coat, a fatherly gesture he had not done for years.

'Yes,' said Ah Choi.

'Trust nobody.'

She nodded.

'And give nobody your name.'

He held her at arm's length, looking at her; but the emotion of the moment overwhelmed her and she fell back into an embrace. 'Father!'

'Be strong,' he whispered.

'I will return. As soon as possible. I promise.'

'Yes. Return to me, Little Bird . . . Return to me.'

She seized his hand and pressed it against her cheek. He smiled but there was an urgency in his voice. He was watching the neighbours' houses, fearful that news of this departure might find its way into official ears.

A flurry of activity down the street alarmed them. 'Go!' urged Father. He drew his hand back. Ah Choi reluctantly turned from him and began to walk. A noise behind her made her turn back. The wooden front door, that was almost always left open day and night, was closing gently. Now she was on her own.

A villager was driving his ox along the street, and all the sights and noises of a new day were beginning. For one last time she surveyed her house, the village and the landscape of her childhood. She would never be anonymous here again, never be the attractive university graduate for whom the Cadre had a romantic eye. From now on she would be a marked woman: a Christian.

The green singing finch was awake in its cage, singing joyously to greet the new day. Ah Choi took a deep breath, wiped away a last tear, and began her journey.

The Cadre had spent the night in the bushes on the road out of the village. He had not slept at all. His eyes were red in their sockets, rimmed with exhaustion.

To have lost so much in so short a time! He had betrayed the villagers with whom he lived. He would never forget the scenes he had witnessed the previous night, no matter how long he lived. And he had lost the confidence of his superiors: his anguish had been all too clear, and the expression on the Public Security officer's face had been one of exasperation and contempt. It was likely that he would not be trusted again, and worse, that he might not have heard the last of the whole business by any means.

But the hollowness sitting inside him, the ache in his heart, was caused by something much deeper. What had occupied the Cadre's thoughts, brooding through the long hours of darkness, was the realization that he had destroyed his own integrity. He was no longer the guardian of the village Communism, leading his people on the narrow path to Socialist truth. Now he was nothing better than a thug and a murderer. Other hands had wielded the clubs that wounded the women and children, but it was he who had ordered them to. Nobody would have done anything if he had not given the word.

Somebody was walking along the path, a slight figure carrying a satchel, a straw sun hat slung across her shoulders. He emerged from the bushes, rubbing his eyes. Ah Choi was walking towards him, walking quickly as if pursued. He looked at the satchel. He groaned inwardly, knowing what was in the bag.

While she was still some distance away she saw him and for a moment slowed down, then thought better of it and made to hurry past him. He called out to her.

'If you leave, your chances of a good placement will be destroyed,' he said, not unkindly. Her pace did not change. 'Ah Choi,' he pleaded, 'there is no turning back. If you leave now you'll never be able to return.'

She stopped, but did not turn to face him. He continued his verbal assault, desperate to make her change her mind.

'You will be a fugitive!'

She still did not turn round. 'I am prepared for that,' she said calmly.

'Are you?' The Cadre's voice was sceptical. 'Are you prepared to spend your whole life running from the law? Sleeping on floors, living like a common beggar off other people's charity? Are you really prepared to throw your whole life away – for this?'

She turned to face him. 'No, Cadre. I am not throwing it away, I have found it. I have found my life!'

'And what happens when they take it from you?' demanded the Cadre bitterly. 'Your cause is that of a fool, Ah Choi. Nobody can oppose our government. Anybody who tries will be destroyed. *You* will be destroyed.' *How different a life you would have had with me*, he thought, *if all this nonsense had not turned your head*.

'Perhaps,' she said.

He stared at her, not understanding.

'Cadre, do you see those bamboo trees over here? Do you see how green and fresh they are?'

He looked at the bamboo then, blankly, back at her. She continued, 'It makes no different how cold the winter is, nor how many times the bamboo is cut down. The bamboo always comes back, stronger, greener. And it always comes back much more full of . . . life.'

She turned to face him fully. 'Life, Cadre! That's what I was searching for – and that is what I have found.' She reached into the satchel. 'And it is a life that is available to anybody, Cadre. *Anybody*.' She held out a Bible to him, her face glowing with a certainty he had not seen in her before.

He contemplated the Bible, taken aback by her boldness, as he so often had been in the past. His gaze travelled between the pamphlet and Ah Choi and back again. Then, almost mechanically, he reached out his hand and took it. His eyes never left her face.

She shouldered the satchel again and resumed her path. The Cadre looked down at the pamphlet: it was like many he had seen before. Maybe this time he would read it. He watched Ah Choi as she walked on, to a future dark with possible persecution, suffering and fear. He almost envied her.

Cho Ling sat down in the suddenly empty house. Lost in thought, he poured himself a glass of wine, but as he raised it to his lips he suddenly stopped, placed it back on the table and looked at it thoughtfully. Then he replaced the cap on the bottle and went to the cupboard to put it away.

As he opened the drawer he saw a book that had not been there before. It was one of the Preacher's New Testaments, obviously placed there by Ah Choi.

He looked down at it for a long time, then hesitantly reached out for it, touching it reverently with his fingers. He felt its texture, the crackle of the pages, and memories of other times came flooding back. He remembered what he had once had, and what some day he might have again.

Out on the road beyond the edge of the village, Ah Choi was still walking, a lone small dot climbing out of the limitless sea of bamboo, up high into the mountains. As she walked, the tall fronds of the trees below swayed and danced, as if the land itself was alive and rejoicing.

POSTSCRIPT:
TWO YEARS LATER

In a village much like Ah Choi's, but many miles distant from it, the villagers were at work in the fields. The men were planting seedlings while the mothers and children slowly worked their way down the trenches, clearing away weeds and obstructions that might block the flow of water from the irrigation channels. It was cool and overcast, and the public loudspeaker nearby broadcasting an exhortation to labour and productivity did not add much cheerfulness to a day in which nobody was taking very much pleasure in anything.

An elderly woman stood up painfully, rubbing the small of her back. She looked around her and stretched luxuriously. About to stoop back to work, she stood up again suddenly and nudged her neighbour. 'Who's that?' she demanded.

A figure was approaching along the rutted cart track leading to the village, a young woman wearing practical, plain clothes. Her hair was knotted back from her tanned face in a businesslike fashion and across her shoulders she carried a heavy bag. 'I don't recognize her,' said the neighbour. 'She's not from round here.'

The newcomer sat down on the edge of the field and gratefully took the burden from her back. A small group of interested children approached, and their mothers followed, ostensibly to fetch the children back but in reality as curious as their offspring. 'Hello,' smiled the visitor to the nearest children. She greeted the adults shyly, but with a quiet authority.

'There are Christians here, I've heard.'

A woman pushed forward. 'Yes! I'm a believer. And so is she – and she – and she is one of us too . . .' Soon the small group was bigger.

'I would like to ask permission to stay in the village for a time. I have walked here from____' She named a village seventy miles away. 'I would like to talk to you about Jesus, and speak with those who are not believers.' She massaged her shoulders, where the canvas bag had scored red weals in her flesh. 'I have Bibles, teaching materials.'

A murmur of excitement ran through the group as she continued. 'I will only stay if you wish me to.'

'Of course we want you to stay! Have you had any food today?'

'They had no food at____. And it was not possible for me to stay at the village. So I came straight here, where I would have come next anyway.' She spoke without rancour, though her feet were cut and aching and her stomach was cramped for lack of nourishment.

The older women gasped in sympathy. Two of them disappeared into one of the houses to get some food for the visitor. Not far from the group a swarthy man, dressed differently from the others, was edging closer to listen to their conversation, not troubling to conceal his interest. One of the women nodded in his direction. 'Our Cadre. We need to be careful.' They instinctively lowered their voices.

'Tell us your name,' demanded another. 'And where is your home? Are you a teacher? And how did you come to know the Lord Jesus?'

With a contented smile, Ah Choi began to tell her story.

THE CHRISTIAN CHURCH IN CHINA

I

Over one-fifth (21.98%) of all the people in the world live in China; its population of around 1,042,000,000 – annual growth 1.1% – makes it by far the largest nation in the world. Geographically it is the world's third largest state with an area of 9,561,000 sq. km., not including Taiwan, Hong Kong and Macao. Over 70% of the population live in the rural areas.

There are eight major languages and 600 dialects, but only one written language. The educational reforms of the Marxist regime have produced 76% literacy.

II

The history of the Christian Church in China is a story of alternating encouragement and persecution. Often Christians were valued for the contribution they made to Chinese society (for example in medicine), and in earlier periods the Church made common cause with the Asian powers against the threat of Islam; but often, too, Christianity was seen as the tool of Western and other foreign interests that threatened the isolationism favoured by China for much of its history. Today, Christianity, though officially tolerated, is seen by the Marxist regime to be (with all other religions) irrelevant to the needs and future of the Chinese state.

Christianity reached China as early as the seventh century, when the Nestorians (an early missionary sect) spread out along the trade routes of Central Asia, reaching central China by AD 635. Probably because it was largely monastic with limited influence, this first Chinese Church declined; by the end of the tenth century it was reported by travellers that there was no trace of Christianity in the Chinese empire.

By the thirteenth century, the Church had once again established itself in many parts of Asia. Ambassadors were sent to the Great Khan by the pope, urging him to adopt Christianity. In 1294 a papal ambassador reached Beijing where he established a church and was later made bishop. The fortunes of the Church fluctuated. In the following century further papal ambassadors arrived but the Church in China again declined. The last Christians were expelled from Beijing in 1369.

China then remained closed to the Gospel until the sixteenth century, when Matthew Ricci, a Jesuit missionary, had a vision to evangelize the country. He was permitted to enter Beijing in 1600, where he stayed for ten years building a small church (about 2,000 members in 1610) which was allowed to exist by favour of the emperor.

By the time of Ricci's death the mission was well established, and further missions had been founded in Shanghai, Chekiang and Hangchow. Even the fall of the Ming dynasty in 1662 did not affect the Church, and, with some occasional setbacks, it flourished.

During the eighteenth century the Russian Church sent missionaries to China. They were active throughout the century, though always less numerous than the Catholic missions. The Jesuits, however, declined during the same period. The Church had always existed according to the favour of the emperor, and increasing tensions between Beijing and Rome led to an expulsion of all provincial missionaries in 1724. The Jesuits in Beijing were permitted to continue, but by 1800 only a handful of Christians remained in the capital.

III

The first Protestant missionary, Robert Morrison, arrived in Canton in 1807 where he lived – marginalized from the vast area of mainland China – for twenty-five years, producing a Chinese dictionary and a translation of the Bible. His strategy was to evangelize expatriate Chinese people, as mainland China was still closed to the Gospel. Like William Carey, he gave education a high priority in his mission strategy and founded the Anglo-Chinese College in 1818.

The Treaty of Nanking in 1842, which brought the First Opium War to an end, effectively re-opened China for Western missionaries. While many Christians had considerable doubts about the Treaty and the war itself, and the perceived links between Western military aggression and the entry of the Gospel rankled in the minds of many Chinese for many years afterwards, the new opportunities were marked by a massive increase in missionary work – Roman Catholic missions expanding faster than Protestant – and some setbacks and misunderstandings. (It was during this period that the notorious Gutzlaff was active – he was a missionary who was found to be employing workers heavily involved in armed drug running.)

In 1853 the English evangelical James Hudson Taylor came to China. He was twenty-one years old and was sent by the Chinese Evangelization Society. In his first seven years he learned Chinese, married, embarked on extensive travels within the country, and finally resigned from the

Society and determined to look to God alone as his director and supporter in mission.

Hudson Taylor's great contribution to mission was his decision to dress like the Chinese, in an attempt to identify with them. It was a move that increased the criticism that his unconventional methods attracted. In 1860 he returned to England because of ill-health. Far from abandoning his missionary call, however, in 1865 he founded – on his own initiative – the China Inland Mission, whose principles of operation (interdenominational, not demanding high education, administratively based in China rather than London, etc.) were a new departure in missionary society practice. One of the principles was that missionaries would wear Chinese dress.

The new Society was immediately successful, with large numbers of applicants. Within thirty years 641 C.I.M. missionaries were working all over China, often in pioneering and dangerous situations. They included both relatively uneducated missionaries and intellectuals such as the 'Cambridge Seven'. One of the great strengths of the C.I.M. was its effectiveness in co-ordinating a membership that covered a wide spectrum of education and churchmanship.

Bishop Stephen Neill was drawn a distinction[1] between the 'diffusion' policy of the C.I.M. – preaching the Gospel to anybody who would listen – and the policy of 'concentration', which targeted the scholar class in China, a country that venerated scholarship, and held that converts from that class would be far more effective missionaries to their countrymen than any foreign missionary could be. Missionary enterprises of this kind included the Society for the Diffusion of Christian and General Knowledge

[1] Stephen Neill, *A History of Christian Missions* (Penguin Books, 1964), p. 336.

among the Chinese, and the movement for creating Christian universities in China.

At the end of the nineteenth century the activities of both Protestants and Roman Catholic missionaries were viewed by Chinese traditionalists as Western penetration of Chinese society. The period was one in which traditionalist and Westernizing tendencies in China were already in tension, and missionaries were the victims of increasing harassment and attacks as the century came to an end. The Roman Catholic missionaries suffered particularly.

What precipitated a mood into a crisis was the attitude of the Dowager Empress, who became a figurehead for the traditionalist forces, and publicly endorsed the violent, anti-foreigner Boxer movement. In 1900 an edict was issued from Beijing calling for the murder of all foreigners. It was a period of appalling atrocities against Christians: probably 30,000 Chinese Roman Catholics and 1,900 Chinese Protestants lost their lives. 188 Protestant missionaries and 47 expatriate Roman Catholic priests also died at the hands of the Boxers. For fifty-five days the foreign legations were beseiged in Beijing: it was there during this period that the great evangelist Wang Mingdao was born.

The Boxer Rising was put down by foreign powers who came to rescue their legation. In the years that followed, the Church grew and missionary work flourished. Of this period, too, it may be said that the believers were like the bamboo. A period of relative toleration came to an end with the revolution ten years later and the founding of the Chinese republic.

The early years of the twentieth century were times of political turmoil for China, with the Republic of China first unsuccessfully founded in 1911, and the missionaries were increasingly threatened. Some easing of the situation came with the conversion and baptism of Chiang Kai Shek in 1930. Chiang was the leader of the dominant

Kuomintang faction. But in 1937 Japan invaded China, and the country entered a period of terrible suffering which lasted until 1945. It was a crisis period for the Church, which lost lives and property, but also continued to work and evangelize, besides providing shelter and medicine.

During the Japanese occupation the Christian community suffered but also grew. There were many opportunities for the Gospel: some missionaries entered China from Japan, and there was considerable outreach among the refugees that flooded into China after Japan's entry into the Second World War in 1941. The suffering of the Church during this period contributed to its growing character and strength; as so often in its history, it was deprived of support from outside and had to grow spiritually and strategically solely under the direction of God.

When the Japanese were driven out in 1945 the Communists staged a coup against the Kuomintang regime, arguing that it was incompetent to deal with the social and economic problems faced by the country. On 1 October 1949 The People's Democratic Republic of China was formally constituted in Beijing and Chiang Kai Shek fled with his supporters to Taiwan.

IV

For many Chinese the Communist victory was a rebirth of national dignity after centuries of subjection to Western interests and Japan. To some extent this is reflected in the Three-Self Patriotic Movement and the Catholic Patriotic Association.

The former was officially launched in 1951, its leaders chiefly theologically liberal and Communist sympathizers: its first chairman was an avowed Marxist Communist, Wu Yaozong, who soon closed down all other Protestant Christian organizations and embarked on a programme of

Church consolidation. It was, as its name suggests, a wholly Chinese movement with no links with any foreign Church or agency (Self governing; Self supporting; Self propagating). It is technically a 'people's organization', but takes its direction from the Chinese Community Party.[2] For such reasons the leading Evangelical evangelist in Beijing, Wang Mingdao, refused to join: in 1955 a nationwide accusation campaign was launched against him.

The Catholic equivalent of the Three-Self Patriotic Movement, the Catholic Patriotic Association, was founded in 1950 to great resentment from the Catholic clergy, and from the outset symbolized a conflict between the ruling Chinese authorities and the See of Rome.

Both had been subverted and controlled within ten years of the founding of the People's Republic with its agenda that included the total elimination of all religious life in China. While there are undoubtedly some committed believers among its clergy, the activities of the Three-Self Patriotic Movement documented in Tony Lambert's *The Resurrection of the Chinese Church* account for the vitriolic attack made upon the visiting Three-Self Patriotic Movement pastor by Amah: failure to support persecuted believers, reports of extortion of money in return for permission to hold communion services, attacks on Christians receiving Christian books from overseas, and more.

The culmination of the Marxist programme was the Cultural Revolution of 1966–76. It was a period of appalling persecution of believers and intellectuals, with huge loss of life. Bibles were publicly burned, churches were vandalized and often demolished, and any manifestation of Christianity – a cross or even a Christmas card – made its owner the target of harassment and persecution.

---

[2] Cf. Tony Lambert, *The Resurrection of the Chinese Church* (Hodder & Stoughton, 1991), p. 53.

Religious activity of all kinds had to go underground, and believers were ridiculed and publicly humiliated. The experiences of Ah Choi's parents as described in the film were typical. Mao died in 1976 and soon afterwards the extreme left-wing Gang of Four who had masterminded the Cultural Revolution were toppled.

The collapse of the demagogic Mao cult, with its distinctly religious overtones – the Little Red Book that was venerated by millions, the obeisance to Mao as the Great Helmsman, the widespread belief that Mao was probably immortal – opened many hearts for a consideration of the claims of Christianity. Just as Ah Choi was to discover twenty years later, a yawning gap had been exposed in China's soul: the spiritual charisma of Maoism had given way to a sense of disillusionment in which the Gospel found a ready hearing in many quarters. Of course, the Three-Self Patriotic Movement's collusion with the authorities and its confessedly tolerant attitude to atheistic Marxism-Leninism created anger among believers that Amah, for one, never forgot, though during the Cultural Revolution the Three-Self churches were also attacked. It was the boast of the revolutionaries that religion was now dead in China.

In the period of reconstruction that followed, the Three-Self Patriotic Movement and the Catholic Patriotic Association were rehabilitated and in 1978 allowed more freedom. The primary reason was to help the healing of Chinese society in the turmoil following the Cultural Revolution, but both organizations were identified by the authorities in Beijing as effective tools for gaining state control over religion and eventually exterminating it.

One major result of the new profile of the Three-Self Patriotic Movement was the re-opening of churches and the granting of permission for believers to reclaim Christian premises that had been allocated for other uses. However, much earlier – from the early 1950s – believers had begun to abandon the state-tolerated churches and meet in private homes. By the late 1980s the house church movement in China was well established: in 1986 it was estimated that of 45,000,000 Protestant Christians, over two-thirds were members of house churches. In 1991 David Aikman cited growth from about 3,000,000 Roman Catholics and less than 1,000,000 Protestants in 1949, to a total in 1991 of between 40 and 60 million. Of these, the Three-Self Patriotic Movement numbers its membership of Protestant and Catholics independent from Rome as 6,000,000.[3]

Harassment and persecution of house churches has been continuous. For example in 1983 the Anti-Spiritual Pollution Campaign was launched, resulting in many arrests of house-church leaders and some attempt at 're-education' of some of those arrested. The numbers of those arrested is not known, but disturbing reports have appeared indicating that the Campaign was used as an instrument of penalizing those who refused to join the Three-Self Patriotic Movement. The Public Security Bureau is the instrument for carrying out the wishes of the Three-Self Patriotic Movement: the Cadre in *Bamboo in Winter* would have had no illusions about the probable results of passing information to the Bureau about the Preacher's activities.

As this book goes to press there are indications that the situation remains essentially the same for China's Christians. Indeed, there are reports of a tightening of religious policy since the failed Soviet coup in 1991.

The long-term vision of Marxism-Leninism, however – the eventual extermination of all religion – is as far from realization as it ever was. Over the past forty years there

[3] David Aikman, 'China's House Church Christians: Still Underground' (review of Ken Anderson's *Bold as a Lamb*), *NNI Review* (10 October 1991), p. 4.

have been many Chinese revivals. Since 1977 many millions have become Christians. Tens of thousands of believers meet in house churches, and even in the state-manipulated Three-Self Patriotic Movement churches there are many godly pastors and committed believers. Over 4,000 churches have been re-opened and there are over 30,000 meeting points for the movement. And all this has happened in a period when foreign missionaries have been forbidden to operate in China.

As the ideologies of the past fail and the people grow disillusioned with their leaders, there is a hunger in China which is being satisfied as thousands turn to God. Ah Choi's story concerns just one individual and her family; but it is a story that is being repeated a millionfold in China today.

EVANGELISM IN CHINA: MASS MEDIA EVANGELISM IN THE WORLD'S LARGEST STATE

Any comment on evangelism in China has to be read in conjunction with the fact that the population of China is increasing at the rate of approximately 12 million people each year – which, as David Bonavia points out, is 'a figure equivalent to the entire population of Australia'.[4] Though the population growth has been slowed down and even reversed in some areas, in others the population has continued to grow, sometimes at a faster rate than food production. Such figures are a reminder that though the preaching of the Gospel has, under God, flourished amazingly in recent years and in often unpromising circumstances, the harvest field is an enormous one and much remains to be done. Some one billion Chinese people remain unreached by the Gospel.

Evangelism is the communication of the Gospel, and in China the communications and media revolution has been a major feature – and indeed a major tool – of the social transformation of the postwar years. Radio, television and news media have all made rapid progress in China. And all are being used in the preaching of the Gospel.

In 1985 ownership of television stood at 50,000,000 –

[4] David Bonavia, *The Chinese: a Portrait* (Penguin Books, Rev. edn 1989), p. 9.

one set for every 20 Chinese. There are 216,000,000 radio receivers, and in rural villages such as Ah Choi's in *Bamboo in Winter* at least one public address loudspeaker would be connected into the local radio network. The radio audience, according to a survey of listeners in 1982, is about 98.3% in Beijing and 93.3% in the rural areas. Corresponding expansion of cinema and video industries has taken place. At the same period China had 1,632 newspapers, with one person in seven having a copy of a newspaper.[5]

The various resources used by the Preacher in his work are only some of a wide range used to preach the Gospel in China today. *Cassette tapes*, including study material, Christian songs and Scripture readings, are very popular in a country that in 1984 contained 10,000,000 cassette players. Christian tape material is produced by organizations both inside China and aboard. *Christian broadcasting* has also been extremely successful. Each month over 2,300 hours of broadcasting in five languages are transmitted to China. The Far East Broadcasting Corporation, Transworld Radio and the Far East Broadcasting Association all have extensive China-orientated broadcasting. A major correspondence ministry exists – for example, over 50,000 letters were received from radio listeners between 1979 and 1984. It has been suggested that half of all conversions have been, at least in part, due to Christian radio broadcasts. *Christian literature* is scarce and much sought-after; many Western publishers have produced Chinese editions of Christian titles. For example a Chinese translation of Lion Publishing's *Handbook to the Bible* was published in 1980 by the Hong Kong company Christian Communications Ltd and has sold over 25,000 copies; many other

---

[5] These figures are taken from Ming An-Xiang, 'A statistical survey of developments in China's mass media' (*Media Development* 1/1986), pp. 13–14.

Lion titles have been translated including the *Encyclopaedia of the Bible* (Tien Dao, 1982) and the *Children's Bible* (Tien Dao, 1988). Lion are only one of a number of Christian publishers active in this way.

Categories of literature particularly needed are hymn books, Bible study and teaching materials, biographies, tracts and apologetic writings aimed at presenting the Gospel to intellectuals. (For example Lion's *Bible Map Book*, Cross Hong Kong 1987, and several titles in the Lion Pocket Book series have been much used in evangelism: Michael Green's *Ten Myths About Christianity* and Norman Warren's *What's the Point* have both been extensively distributed.)

The student community is open to the Gospel in a number of ways. For example China's current policy of fostering links with the West for the purpose of its own survival has meant that there is a continuous exposure to Western influences, to some extent. Hundreds of thousands of people visit China, admittedly often under strict supervision and on the government's terms, but Westerners are not the bizarre aliens in China that they were in some previous centuries; students and intellectuals are likely to be the social group most affected by such exposure. In addition many Westerners come to China to study and over 40,000 Chinese students leave for further education overseas each year; they come back with a wider perspective than they had when they left. The final appendix in this book reprints an article that provides information on Christianity and intellectuals in modern China.

As a woman, Ah Choi would have access both to university education and the mass media. In the 1950s the Constitution of New China had guaranteed women equal rights in political, economic and educational fields.

With the rapid development in rural areas, more people began to see what changes an education can bring to their lives. One indication of the success of this programme is the large number of periodicals available in the country, including a political journal called *Women*.

Many women work in the fields and sideline enterprises, while their husbands leave home to run the businesses. Those with some schooling or junior or middle school graduates always progressed quickly. Today, rural residents anxiously seek technical guidance and collect funds to build and expand schools.[6]

But recent events in China have created a unique openness among Chinese intellectuals. Following the death of up to 3,000 students and citizens in Tiananmen Square, there is a widespread conviction that the state ideology has turned against its own members and is intellectually and spiritually bankrupt. According to Anthony Lambert (script consultant to *Bamboo in Winter* and author of *The Resurrection of the Chinese Church*, Hodder and Stoughton, 1991) the period following the Tiananmen Square massacre has seen a decline in Party membership and a massive increase in church affiliations, including the Three-Self Patriotic Movement. Ah Choi's disillusionment and deep spiritual hunger are typical of the feelings of numerous young Chinese students and other intellectuals: Lambert quotes a young Party member as saying that after the 4 June 1989 massacre he 'no longer believed in anything'.

The opposition of the district authorities to the teaching of the Preacher reflects the situation in China today (an illuminating real-life account can be found in Ron McMillan's article reproduced below). For example restrictions

[6] 'Wiping Out Illiteracy' in *Women of China* (May 1985).

issued in Anhui in 1989 – called the 'Six Don'ts' – forbade
Christians to correspond with Hong Kong, listen to
foreign radio broadcasts, take up collections, spread
Christianity outside the church building, or set up unofficial house churches. The Preacher's meetings in Ah
Choi's village would be regarded as setting up an unofficial
– because non-Three-Self – house meeting. Much evangelical Christian work is regarded as transgressing the
fundamental principles of the Three-Self Patriotic Movement (self-government, self-support, self-propagation).
The Chinese Communist Party exercise a strong control
on the Church so that the three 'selfs' are in practice
often purely nominal, but in that situation the Church has
grown enormously with widespread revival and church
planting.

Anthony Lambert in a recent article[7] quotes an internal
Party document that:

> lamented the fact that there were more than 7,700
> itinerant evangelists known to the authorities in just
> 13 of China's 30 provinces, and blamed the growth
> of the Chinese Church from 700,000 in 1949 to over
> 5 million registered members today squarely on the
> evangelistic zeal of these itinerants. In fact, there is
> good evidence pointing to a conservative estimate of
> more than 20 million Protestant Christians in China
> today.

The film *Bamboo in Winter* revolves around the activities
of an unnamed itinerant evangelist. In a sense the twentieth
century has been the century of evangelism in China, for
the efforts of evangelists have led to a number of revivals.
For example the independent ministry of John Sung

[7] Tony Lambert, 'China Crisis' (*Alpha*, August 1991), pp. 19–21.

(1901–44) extended widely through China and south-East Asia in the 1920s, as he preached against hypocritical living and challenged his hearers to turn to Christ. His ministry is described by Tony Lambert as 'perhaps the most extraordinary ministry [of the period] appointed by God'.

Perhaps the most famous Christian evangelist is Wang Mingdao, the 'man of iron', born in 1900 in the palace of Prince Su, a protector of Christians. He became a preacher at the age of 22, edited the magazine *Spiritual Food Quarterly*, and in 1950 was attacked by leaders of the Three-Self Patriotic Movement, which he had opposed. He was arrested in August 1954, and so was his wife. He was sentenced to a labour camp in 1970 and was released in 1979. In his early ministry he built his own Evangelical Tabernacle in Beijing, and became widely influential. He died in 1991. The work of John Sung and Wang Mingdao, and many like them both well-known and obscure, laid spiritual foundations in the years prior to 1949 that were to sustain the Church through years of suffering.

A WEEKEND IN THE LIFE OF A CHINESE ITINERANT EVANGELIST

BY RON MACMILLAN
Asia Correspondent for News Network International,
1987–91

Itinerant evangelists have always been crucial to the growth of the church in China. Dr John Sung was an itinerant evangelist all his life, and Church statesman Wang Mingdao began this way before settling into a ministry in Beijing.

However, since 1949 the growth of the itinerant evangelists has become crucial to the vitality and growth of the Christian community . . . albeit more difficult.

The mere fact of being an independent itinerant evangelist is to be a lawbreaker on at least two counts: the constitution states that evangelism must take place only within designated religions premises, and preachers must be accredited by the local Protestant Three-Self organization.

With travel as difficult as it is in China, mass communications so primitive, and the population so immobile, the traditional way of the travelling preacher spreading the Word is still the main way of proclaiming the Gospel. And so thousands volunteer for a life of hardship and stress. Most itinerants in China are young, uneducated men and women, so the central character in our report is not typical in this respect. However, the hectic lifestyle, the sacrificial availability to people, and the ever present danger, is very typical.

Brother Jonah is a close associate of the recently arrested Li Tien En.* A Hong Kong Chinese Christian spent a weekend

---

* Li Tren En is no longer under police arrest.

with him last year, and NNI Asia Correspondent Ron MacMil-
lan now retells the story of that eventful period through the eyes
of Brother John's weekend companion.

Itinerant evangelists are 'go anywhere, do anything'
people. One of the history's greatest itinerant preachers,
John Wesley, said that the true itinerant needed only four
characteristics to be successful: 'a back for any bed, a face
for any weather, a stomach for any food, and strength for
any work'.

It may seem a rather physical definition, but then few
are witnesses to the hectic and exhausting lifestyle of a real
itinerant evangelist. One such individual is Brother Jonah,
a native of Shanghai, who has been an itinerant preacher
throughout the length and breadth of China since 1976.
He maintains a schedule that a twenty-year-old would find
exhausting. Brother Jonah is seventy-three.

We first join up with Jonah in Shanghai. He is collecting
a huge pack of Bibles and spiritual books from a friend to
take into the interior. The red, blue and white bag weighs
60 pounds, bending his slight frame almost to the ground
as he shoulders it. He staggers off to the railway station
where he buys a single ticket to a town in Henan province.
It is the last of his money. He will eat nothing on the
twenty-hour journey.

Sitting amid the clamour of a third-class carriage, he
confides the nature of his expedition to me. 'I received a
request to preach the Gospel in the village of X. Appar-
ently someone was converted under my ministry else-
where, and he has returned to his home village, where he
finds he is the only believer in 500 people.'

As Jonah talks, the people crammed around him try to
listen. He is wedged between two young men on the
wooden seat, two soldiers stand in the crowded aisle, and
a family of three occupy the bench opposite. They all look

at him, a small man dressed in a drab and shabby Mao suit of dark blue. I begin to fret to myself: 'Is something wrong?'

The soldier can restrain himself no longer. He leans forward and says, 'Old man, tell us why you seem so happy?'

Jonah is a master at drawing people out, so he replies with a question: 'What do you think? What do you think would be the happiest thing that could ever happen to you, and I'll tell you whether that has happened to me.'

He addressed the question to all who were listening. The suggestions came thick and fast. The young woman sitting opposite said, 'A big house would make me the happiest person in the world.' The younger man next to Jonah said, 'No, I just want to be loved by a beautiful and wonderful woman.' Said another, 'I'd like a passport to America,' and one of the soldiers shouted, 'If I had the power to command the People's Liberation Army I should be the happiest man in the world.'

A broad grin spread across Jonah's face at all this. They asked, 'Do you have any of these? Is that why you are so happy?'

'Yes!' Jonah replied. 'I have all of them, and more.'

They drew back aghast. He smiled again. They hung on his every word. 'Let me see now,' he said impishly. 'I have a mansion so large an emperor would be green with envy; I am loved devotedly by the most beautiful person in the world; I have the perfect freedom to go wherever I wish; and I happen to be a very close friend of the most powerful man on earth.'

He went on, 'In fact, I have received all this from one person, and his name is Jesus Christ.' To my surprise, there was no visible change of expression at the mention of Jesus. In the West one expects derision or shock. Here there was only insatiable curiosity.

For twenty hours Jonah talked. It was a night train, but he talked all night. He pulled out his frayed Bible and took them through it book by book. I kept dozing off, but on he went, hunched over his Bible, talking in earnest tones to his still-eager audience.

As dawn broke we reached our destination. Jonah delved into his backpack and distributed New Testaments and tracts. He shook hands warmly with all of them, and we stepped out into the frosty morning.

'I believe they are not far from the kingdom,' he said. 'All but one of them were greatly convicted by God, but the fellow sitting beside me could spell trouble.' As if on cue, the same man passed us on the station platform. He gave us both a long look.

Suddenly we were approached by another man of about 30. 'Praise the Lord,' he said, looking at Jonah: 'God has answered my prayers and sent you.' He took us out to the front of the station and pointed to three rusty bicycles. 'Our transport,' he said cheerily. 'It's a five-hour ride to my village.'

So the three of us set off into the vast plain that dominates Henan Province. How Jonah managed to balance on the bike with that heavy bag was quite beyond me – nor how he had the strength to keep pedalling and talking at the same time, for the young man was full of questions and Jonah patiently answered them all.

Three hours into the journey I pulled alongside him with my aching legs and joked, 'It's a miracle that you are fit enough to do this at your age.'

'That's exactly what it is,' came the very serious reply.

He late confided, 'It's at those times that I feel the strength of the Lord more than at any other time, because the hardest thing is to be constantly available to people when you are extremely tired.' He also added, 'Of course, it did help that the ground was flat.'

We arrived at the village mid-morning. To my surprise, most of the village residents were at home, but the it was not the season to be out in the fields.

I didn't have to wonder for long how Jonah would gather a crowd to start preaching. He simply dived into a house, came out with two large tin pots, and proceeded to bang them together. He shouted over the din, 'Friends, come and hear about a God who can really transform your life!' They came running, and he had his audience five minutes after arriving at the village.

A student of homiletics would have little to learn from Jonah's sermon, and much to be appalled at, but he communicated nevertheless. He spoke for fifty minutes about his biblical namesake, Jonah. He said that their little village in China had two things in common with the huge important city of Nineveh; first, that it was full of people who were living their lives in ignorance and defiance of the one true God, and second, that the true God would judge the inhabitants soon if they did not repent.

The 200 villagers listened with rapt attention. It was a totally new teaching to them. Jonah later explained, 'Chinese people just gape with astonishment when they are told that what is wrong with the world is themselves.' He added, 'All China's religions, right up to Mao's "religion", affirm that human beings are basically good, it's the circumstances that make them bad. So when they hear that they are the ones that are bad, it is a totally new concept that they can hardly take in.'

Jonah went on to tell them about the love God had for them, and wept tears as he told them of the sufferings Jesus endured on the cross. Then he led them in a prayer of repentance. About a quarter of the villagers said the prayer with him. The kingdom of God had come at last to this poor village.

I did not see Jonah for the rest of the afternoon. He was

spending time with three converts, two men and a
woman. He had selected them to lead the new church and
was busy giving them a crash course in Christian doctrine.
Leaving them a stock of Bibles from his backpack, he
exhorted them, 'Do nothing hastily, do nothing out of
anger. Every decision you make should be in accord with
each other, and only after much prayer and searching of
this book.'

As the evening shadows closed in, the peace was
abruptly shattered. Someone had just arrived in the village
on his bicycle saying that the Public Security Bureau was
looking for an evangelist and his companion.

'I knew it,' said Jonah. 'It was that quiet young man on
the train who has informed on us.'

We mounted the bicycles again and pedalled madly after
the villager who had brought us to this place. We went
fast – murderously fast – over rutted roads in the black of
night. After four hours of pedalling we reached a bus
station in a nearby town. There was a bus leaving for one
of the major cities of Henan. But the driver said there was
no room. We pleaded, and he finally relented.

We climbed in and settled in the narrow passageway. It
was an eight-hour ride and all the seats were taken. Jonah
just stretched out lengthwise along the aisle and promptly
went to sleep, waking only when we reached the city
outskirts in the morning.

We didn't realize at the time what a miracle God had
worked to effect our escape. The brother who had invited
Jonah to his village later wrote of it. As he was cycling
back to his village he came across the Public Security
Bureau car. It had run out of petrol barely one mile from
the bus station. He could tell by the heat of the engine
that they had not been stopped long.

'Praise God,' he breathed, and stowed the two extra
bicycles in a nearby hedge before cycling by the stranded

car with its three frustrated occupants. Sure enough, one of them was the young man he had seen looking at Jonah on the platform, who had travelled in the same carriage, and must have been the silent one Jonah had mentioned.

A few weeks later the brother who had reported this incident to us was sitting in a house church in a nearby city when he heard a youth testify to a recent experience. saying: 'I was a petrol pump assistant on duty one night when the local Public Security Bureau car drove in. The driver told me to fill up the tank, and to hurry up about it too. But through the open window I heard that they were en route to arrest an itinerant evangelist who had just arrived that day by train, and was believed to be in X village. Hearing this, I stopped filling the tank. It was probably less than half full, and I prayed that God would blind the driver's eyes from noticing. I'm sure it helped, for I have not heard of any arrest since.'

The youth was able to rejoice with us as the brother explained precisely what happened, as did Jonah and I when we heard of it. 'Won't it be wonderful when we get to heaven and hear about all the other thousands of times God rescued us like this and we never knew?' said Jonah at the time.

Meanwhile we were in this city on a Sunday, and Jonah said, 'We'll go and drop in on a house church leader I know.' After an hour of wandering through the dusty streets of this gray, cheerless city, we reached the leader's home. He was a tall, thin man in his early forties and delighted to see Jonah.

After greeting us his expression became very serious. He began to share: 'We have had a division in our church since you were last here, Jonah. Three of our five elders have led half the church away, and we no longer have fellowship together.'

The church was a large one, comprised of more than

5,000 members in various meeting points. Three thousand were now worshipping with the three renegade elders. 'What was the issue of division?' asked Jonah.

'It has to do with the Lord's return,' was the reply. 'The three elders came under a conviction that the Lord would return in the middle of next year, and that the church should prepare accordingly – sell property, leave jobs, and concentrate more purely on evangelism. The rest of the eldership did not share this conviction, and over a period of months were accused of not showing enough urgency. Eventually the split occurred.'

Jonah said, 'Call all the original elders together for a meeting with me this afternoon.' He had been one of the evangelists instrumental in founding this church, and indeed had selected some of the elders.

That afternoon five elders gathered in the small house. The atmosphere was very tense and strained. I wondered how on earth Jonah would deal with this. What followed was an amazing lesson in Christian reconciliation.

Jonah entered the room and surveyed the group. He said nothing. They looked back. He sat down and looked around him. All of a sudden great sobs heaved his body, tears cascaded down his cheeks, and he cried out in an anguished voice, 'O Lord, how we have dirtied your name!'

His grief, so genuine in its origin and so deep in its extent, broke the strained atmosphere, and soon all the elders were weeping, too. The Holy Spirit seemed to descend on the meeting and we were all filled with the conviction that the Lord's name had been dishonoured. There followed confession, repentance and reconciliation. No words were used. No fingers pointed. No voices raised. No issues aired. Tears were the means, and tears were enough.

Soon it was time to leave and get on the train back to

Shanghai. The elders gave us a gift of money, which happened to be just sufficient to cover the cost of our tickets. But as we prepared to leave the house there was a knock on the door.

To our horror it was the local Party boss. Perhaps he had heard of the meeting with the five elders, and was taking advantage of a fortuitous opportunity to round them up. Or was he after Jonah, who was well known to the authorities as an undesirable in these parts? He said, 'Who is the evangelist Jonah?' Will you come and pray for my eight-year-old son? He is very sick and the doctor does not know what the matter is.'

Amid audible sighs of relief from those present, Jonah replied, 'Why have you come to me? What makes you think I can help?'

'Because I have heard you are in touch with a God of real power,' the Party boss answered simply.

Yet Jonah persisted, 'Why do you think I should be willing to ask God to heal your son? After all, you have not shown much liking for Christians yourself.'

Tension mounted again in the room. Was Jonah going too far? This man was powerful. One word from him and we would be spending the next few months in jail. But it was as though his child's need banished all thoughts of revenge.

'I have also heard that Christians are full of love,' he said, 'and that they forgive their enemies.'

'Do you think that is true?' asked Jonah. 'What possible sense does it make to reach out to enemies in love?'

Speaking with great emotion, the Party boss declared, 'All my life I have been taught to hate – to hate tradition, to hate capitalists, to hate the West, to hate the revisionists. Always the cry is 'Hate, hate, hate'. I know that I have accomplished nothing. And I know that China has gone nowhere. I know that hate only kills. My wife is dead,

my family is dead, and sometimes I feel dead myself.
Hatred has killed them, and it's killing me. But I still feel
love – love for my son – and I know that without that
little love I bear for him, and he for me, I am dead.
Christians are supposed to worship a God of love. Maybe
this God will take pity on my sick son.'

There was a shocked silence in the room. No one had
heard a Party man speak so frankly before.

Jonah said gently, 'We do worship a God of love, and
he is the One who has given you the love you have for
your son. But you don't have to ask me to pray for your
son. Why not speak to God yourself about him?'

'Will he listen to me?' gasped the incredulous Party
cadre.

'Of course,' replied Jonah. 'Now you pray, and we will
pray with you, too.'

Haltingly, the distraught father put together a fragment
of a prayer: 'God, since you are love, save my son, and
free him to live a life of love!'

We all chanted 'Amen' and hurried after him to his son.
Of course we need not have had any anxiety. The boy
was completely well, and two more souls were united in
love to the Lord Jesus Christ.

So we finally made our way back to Shanghai, arriving
late on Monday evening. It had been an amazing weekend.
It had included nine hours of bicycle pedalling, forty hours
on a hard railway seat, and eight hours on a bumpy bus.
Jonah had seen more than fifty Chinese come to the Lord
in a remote village, founded a church, given an all-night
seminar on Bible doctrine to ten eager young people on
the train, reconciled the leaders of 5,000 saints, and converted a high-ranking Party cadre through the healing of
his son – and let us not forget near-capture by the Public
Security Bureau.

Was he tired? He returned to his apartment and sifted

through his mail. Another invitation had arrived from a believer in Gansu Province, requesting him to come and give instruction to 600 full-time workers in a huge house church movement. I later learned he had taken the train to Gansu Province late that same evening.

He once said, 'Rest is for the next world!' Truly, he was a man of his word.

Reprinted from Special Report: a closer look at issues concerning religious liberty worldwide (*11 December 1990*) *with permission from News Network International.*

THE BACKGROUND TO AH CHOI'S STORY: CHINESE INTELLECTUALS AND CHRIST

The role of intellectuals in recent Chinese history is one of the most distinctive characteristics of China's social and religious life. Ah Choi attended Beijing University in the late 1980s, but as Dr Lesley Francis points out, Christian intellectuals have been in confrontation with the authorities since the earliest years of the Communist era in China.

During the mid-1950s, many Christian intellectuals were sent to the countryside and to China's remote border areas. In the cities, a number of Christian intellectuals who refused to join the Three-Self Patriotic Movement (TSPM) were imprisoned, some for 20 years or more.

In the 1960s, during the Cultural Revolution (1966–76), many Christian students and intellectuals were imprisoned. During these years the Church, as an institution, was almost non-existent. It was also during this period that the house church movement began to grow.

Christian Intellectuals in the 1980

In the 1980s there were four distinct groups of intellectuals in China who came to faith in Christ.

There were those who had become Christians in China before the Communist revolution in 1949. Some played prominent roles in urban house churches and most were persecuted for their faith (as well as because they were intellectuals). Many did not trust the government's politics or its umbrella church, the TSPM.

Another group came into the faith prior to 'liberation' (1949) when overseas. Most within this group were taught to lead academic institutions, had excellent English language skills, and were less conservative in their thinking. Some identified with house churches, others with the TSPM.

A third group included those who had travelled overseas in the late 1970s to 1980s and came to to the faith there. On returning to China, however, most did not identify with either the house churches or the TSPM. Until June 4th, 1989, most were extremely cautious of being known as Christians. They lacked fellowship with other Christians and were most likely to trust a foreigner before another Chinese believer.

Lastly, there were those students/intellectuals who became Christians in China, some through Gospel radio broadcasts and others through English language classes taught by foreign Christian professionals. Most were undergraduate students – some very naive about the religious situation in China – and were more open in their faith than the other intellectual Christian groups. Others were very cautious and feared meeting with other Chinese Christians.

Spiritual Awakening in the 1990s
Several factors have contributed to the unprecedented numbers of students and intellectuals embracing Christianity since June 1989. One is the worldwide 'crisis of faith' in Marxism. Chinese authorities have linked the recent spread of Christianity in Eastern Europe with the demise of Communism there.

Another reason for the intellectual revival in China in the 1990s is the perceived inept management of social, economic and political reforms by Chinese authorities. While searching for political reform and democracy, students and intellectuals came into an even more vigorous search for truth. Truth, as an absolute, is not embodied in other Chinese philosophies, eg Buddhism, Taoism (Daoism), Confucianism or Marxism.

Overseas, the response to Christianity since June 1989 has been remarkable. Several key student leaders in the pro-democracy movement who escaped to the West have since become Christians, while many others are attending Bible study groups.

The turning to Christ by Chinese intellectuals in China and their subsequent integration into the Chinese Church is essentially a Chinese phenomenon – and it is continuing.

Recently, a young Chinese university professor, who converted to Christianity in the wake of the Tiananmen Square incident, shared the Gospel with his class of 20 students. Over half the class committed their lives to Christ that day. In another city, a young professor of music was asked to train his students to sing Christmas carols in various hotels. He later shared the Gospel with them and over 20 of his students (from a class of 40) became Christians.

The Chinese Church, however, is still ill-equipped to accommodate and teach these young believers. There are a number of reasons for this: a lack of theologically trained pastors, the low academic standards of those who have been trained in TSPM seminaries, the inability of pastors (in the light of the above points) to answer the questions of the students/intellectuals, the sheer number of new believers, and the lack of materials for discipling the new Christians.

Discipling the New Generation

There are a number of significant factors which point the way to the emergence of Christian student work in the future.

Since June 4, Bible study groups have begun on many Chinese campuses, now joined by undergraduates, graduates, professors and researchers. Also, since mid-1980 there has been a marked growth of Chinese teachers and professors who have become Christians. Throughout a number of Chinese cities, such professors are now supporting and encouraging Christian student groups.

Further, in at least 12 Chinese cities new Christian fellowship groups have been established in the past year. In each case these are Chinese-led with little or no involvement by foreign Christians. Some of these university fellowships are quite large (70–80 students).

Lastly, in several cities there are house church lay persons working exclusively with university students. However, there does not seem to be any Christian student/intellectual structural organization or network, at either the provincial or national level.

There remains a tremendous openness to the Gospel among China's intellectual community. Lack of resources, however, will make the challenge of discipling the intellectual community a critical issue for the Church. The need for Christian literature and apologetic resources written by Chinese Christian intellectuals in simplified Chinese script is critical.

Christians outside of China must now consider creative ways in which to establish a partnership with Chinese Christian intellectuals in order to facilitate their effectiveness in evangelizing and training this new generation of Christian students who are part of the legacy of June 4th, 1989.

(*Abridged, with permission, from* News Network International, *11 June 1991, pp. 31-3. Dr Lesley Francis is the Hong Kong-based director of Overseas Missionary Fellowship's China Study Programme.*)

If you would like to receive further information about 'Open Doors with Brother Andrew' and its ministry to the Suffering Church worldwide, please write to us.

Upon request we shall gladly send you – free of charge – our monthly magazine, which gives up-to-date news and information about persecuted Christians around the world.

Name: ....

Address: ....

Town: ....

Postal Code: ....

Country: ....

Forward this form to:

Open Doors	Open Doors	Open Doors International
P.O. Box 6	Box 27001	P.O. Box 47
Witney	Santa Ana	3840 AA Harderwijk
Oxon	CA 92799	The Netherlands
OX8 7SP	USA	
England		